SURVIVING THE GREAT RESET

A Deep Dive into the New World Order
and What It Means to You from A-Z

STEVE ABBOTT

Table of Contents

Introduction

In 2016, the World Economic Forum published the book The Fourth Industrial Revolution. In it, its founder and CEO Klaus Schwab describes a new era of technological change that is changing the way we live, work, communicate and interact.

He warned that the disruptive shift is happening so quickly that it risks causing widespread social unrest and economic disruption. In the years since this book was published, we have seen this potential become a reality. In particular, the crisis of democracy and the recent (and somehow still ongoing) COVID-19 pandemic has accelerated the pace of change and amplified the devastating effects of the Fourth Industrial Revolution. As a result, we may now be facing an unprecedented global existential crisis. Crisis conflicts that we have never experienced in the past. The crisis has been dubbed the "Great Reset."

This book is your guide to understanding the Great Reset. It's designed to introduce you to certain defining concepts and help you understand what's happening, why it's happening, and how to prepare for the changes to come.

To begin this journey, let's start with a deep dive into the origins of the Great Reset. We'll explore its many facets and the forces that drive it. In Chapter 2, we'll look at the economic aspects of the Great Reset, examine the current economic system and identify some trouble spots to see how the reset will affect your personal finances.

The third chapter is devoted to the social aspects of reset. We'll also talk about current problems in social governance and how the reset will impact your relationships at large. While the fourth chapter will explore the political aspects of the reset, the fifth chapter will have you consider the deeper, spiritual aspects of the reset. In the sixth chapter, we'll look at how we can prepare for it, both mentally and physically.

The seventh chapter will provide useful steps and tips on how to create a lucid Great Reset survival plan. In the eighth chapter, we'll discuss how we can contribute to establishing a new world order based on cooperation, not competition. Lastly, the final chapter will answer some frequently asked questions about the Great Reset. You'll also find a bonus chapter explaining how the reset is already underway.

The Great Reset is happening, whether we're ready for it or not, regardless of how many attempt to resist the change. It's time to wake up and venture deeper into all the intricate and sometimes opaque systems that have come to govern our lives. It's time to take charge of our lives and create a sustainable and desirable future for ourselves and the upcoming generations.

Chapter 1

What Is the Great Reset?

In the coming years, we will witness a paradigm shift in the way we live, work, and play. The Great Reset is a period where both technology and society are set on a new path, one we haven't experienced before. It will be a time of great opportunity and challenge but also a defining moment when it comes to our collective future.

This opening chapter will explore the Great Reset and what it means. We'll take a deep dive into the origins of the concept, what it is, and how it will impact our lives.

The Great Reset

The Great Reset goes far beyond the economic sphere (the domain of markets, exchange, supply and demand, inflation, and deflation cycles...). Initially, the term was coined by Klaus Schwab, an accomplished German engineer, and economist, to describe a new era that began recently with the rise of big data, artificial intelligence (AI), robotics, digital manufacturing technologies, and global networks. Schwab believes that the great reset constitutes the fourth industrial revolution, which is radically different from anything we have experienced before because it will blur the lines between physical objects and human beings, machines and nature, the virtual and the real world.

A paradigm shift occurs when there is a change in the underlying assumptions that govern our actions and decisions. For example, when computers were first invented, they were designed to replace people but they still had to be created by said people. However, once this assumption was questioned, the paradigm shifted: computers could be programmed by using languages like Python and C++. This meant that computers were no longer just tools to perform repetitive tasks faster than humans can; they could think for themselves.

This breakthrough led to computers being used for all sorts of new applications, from controlling industrial machinery to powering air-traffic control systems.

The very same process is at work today, as we gradually shift into a new economic paradigm that will revolutionize our lives and redefine the way we work. The next great economic paradigm will be shaped by new technologies, including AI, robotics, 3D printing, and nanotechnology.

Origins of the Great Reset

The Great Reset is a vast economic transition set to take place over the next 30 to 50 years. It will involve a massive and disruptive transformation of our economic and political systems as we move from an era based on fossil fuels to a new one powered by renewable energy, clean technology, and sustainable growth. This transition will redefine who we are and offer us a chance to redesign our lives.

At the heart of the Great Reset is a crisis, which we have already experienced. In 2008, the world's financial system collapsed due to excessive risk-taking by bankers and investors in the global finance industry. That led to record unemployment worldwide, growing inequality between rich and poor, political turmoil in many countries, and widespread disillusionment with globalization.

The term "Great Reset" was first used by Klaus Schwab in January 2011. During his speech at the World Economic Forum in Davos, Schwab stated that the world is living through a fourth industrial revolution driven by technological advances in cyber-physical systems (robotics), biotechnology, nanotechnology, and quantum computing.

Schwab predicted that this modern revolution would eventually rebalance global political and economic power and lead to social upheaval. He suggested this period of change could be harder to endure than others but would ultimately lead to greater prosperity for society as a whole.

Schwab argued that social inequality would increase during this period and compared it to the changes brought by the first and second industrial revolutions. Schwab predicted there would be a shift in political power from all over the world. We're already witnessing the major geopolitical stakes behind the current war in Ukraine.

Following his speech, Schwab published a report entitled "The Global Agenda," which outlined his vision for how governments should prepare for the future in terms of education and infrastructure. He notably advocated for a number of policies designed to mitigate some of the negative effects of the Fourth Industrial Revolution.

What Does the Great Reset Comprise?

Understanding what a Great Reset is helps to know what led up to it in the first place.

The origins of the Great Reset can be traced back to the Industrial Revolution between 1760 and 1840 when major improvements in technology originated in Europe. With the advent of the steam engine and other innovations in the fields of transportation, mining, and manufacturing, there was a boom in rotary motion, leading to an explosion in mechanical energy.

This produced rapid growth across many industrial sectors, which led to equally rapid growth in wealth for those able to capitalize on it. New jobs were created, and urbanization started as people flocked from rural areas into cities in search of employment opportunities.

However, the fruits of all the labor and value created in the process were not evenly distributed. The rich prospered while the poor were neglected, causing social tension and protests from those who felt they were being exploited. In parallel, there was a sudden rise in income inequality where some countries experienced a greater concentration of wealth than others.

Factors That Led to the Great Reset

The 2008 Financial Crisis

A collapse caused this in the housing market in the United States, which led to a global financial crisis. This had a ripple effect around the world, causing record unemployment, social unrest, and political upheaval. The crisis also led to a loss of confidence in the global financial system due to excessive risk-taking by traders, bankers, and investors.

The market crash of 2008 led to the Great Recession, which lasted from December 2007 to June 2009. This was the biggest and longest economic downturn since the Great Depression of the 1930s. Not only did it have a huge impact on the economy, but it also led to social and political turmoil across all continents.

The Coronavirus Pandemic

This is perhaps the most significant event to occur since the 2008 crisis. The pandemic has resulted in a global health crisis, with over 6,000,000 deaths and counting. It has also caused widespread panic and economic uncertainty, with businesses shutting down and people losing their jobs. The pandemic has also highlighted the shortcomings of our global economic and monetary governance and the need for systemic reforms.

World leaders have called for a Great Reset of the global economy in response to these events. This would involve a rethinking of our economic system, with a focus on sustainability, inclusivity, and equitable growth. The Great Reset would also involve shifting from a consumption-based economy to one based on investments.

The Rise of Automation and Artificial Intelligence

The advancement of technology is pushing towards the automation of many jobs that humans traditionally occupied. This is especially true in the manufacturing sector, where robots are increasingly being used to carry out tasks that were once fully or partially manual.

The boom in artificial intelligence also impacts machines becoming increasingly capable of data analysis and decision-making. The increasing use of algorithms in our everyday lives is also changing the way we interact with the world. With more and more tasks being entrusted to machines, there is a risk of mass unemployment as robots gradually replace humans.

The Impact of Climate Change

Climate change is one of the most significant challenges facing the world today. In fact, the Intergovernmental Panel on Climate Change (IPCC) warned that we have just twelve years to take action to prevent catastrophic temperature increases.

Climate change is already causing extreme weather events, such as floods and droughts, which devastate countless communities around the world. Global warming is also a major threat to our food and water supplies.

Seeing how we need to take urgent action to address climate change, the Great Reset is one way of doing this by shifting the focus of the economy from growth to sustainability.

The Effect on Economic Growth

The world economy has been growing at a slower rate in recent years. This is partly due to the end of the "boom" years following the financial crisis but also to structural problems in the global economy. These include a slowdown in productivity, rising inequality, and an aging population.

The COVID-19 pandemic has exacerbated these already existing issues and is likely to further stall economic growth. This will hurt living standards and could lead to intense waves of social unrest. The world as we know it is facing significant challenges that require fundamental rethinking of the current economic model. The Great Reset is an attempt to do just that.

How Will the Great Reset Impact Our Lives?

The reality many experts and various dedicated researchers are planning is that the Great Reset will profoundly impact our lives. It will redefine who we are and how we live, work, and even relate to one another. Specifically, it will affect our economy and political systems. We will move from an era based on fossil fuels to a new era powered by renewable energy, clean technology, and sustainable growth. This transition will redefine the global population and offer us all a chance to redesign our lives.

The Great Reset will also bring about a new social contract between business, government, and society. This contract will be based on three essential pillars:

Sustainability

We will need to find ways to live within our planet's means and use and allocate resources more efficiently. The norms and values that guide our behavior will need to change. From consumerism to environmentalism, we will have to adopt a more sustainable lifestyle. A key part of this will be the transition to a circular economy, which is estimated to potentially create up to $1 trillion in new business opportunities.

Inclusion

We will need to guarantee everyone a fair chance to participate in and benefit from economic growth. This will require the creation of new jobs, closing the gender pay gap, eliminating inequality, and empowering marginalized groups. It will also require giving everyone access to technology. Achieving this will not be possible without overhauling our education and social welfare systems as they are practiced today (again, with great evident disparities – living and attending school in Norway or Singapore isn't the same in Somalia or Afghanistan).

Diversity

We will need to embrace diversity in all its forms. This includes cultural, ethnic, and religious diversity and the diversity of thought and freedom of opinion. We will need to find ways to respect and value our differences while recognizing our shared humanity. The Great Reset will require us to build bridges instead of walls.

Impact on Individual Lives

On a personal level, the Great Reset will challenge us to rethink our values and, generally, how we live our lives. It will force us to consider the real value of what we tend to take for granted, such as our jobs, homes, and even our identities.

The way we work will change. With the rise of automation and artificial intelligence, many jobs that have existed for centuries will disappear. This will create both opportunities and challenges, and tens of millions of people will need to find new ways to make a living.

The way we live will also change, as we will need to come up with ways to live within our planetary boundaries and manage our resources more efficiently. This will require us to adopt a more sustainable and forward-thinking lifestyle.

The Great Reset will also affect our relationships. We will need to find ways to connect in a more meaningful way. How we relate to each other will also need to change.

Impact on the World

Some people have called for a "great reset" of the world economy in the wake of the Coronavirus pandemic. The idea is that this crisis presents an opportunity to build a fairer, more sustainable world. The Great Reset would involve major changes to the way we live and work, such as introducing a universal basic income, decarbonizing the economy, and rethinking our approach to globalization.

Supporters argue that the Great Reset is a once-in-a-generation opportunity to build a better world. Critics, however, say that it is naive to think that we can simply reset the world after this crisis. Instead, they argue that the Great Reset will only benefit corporations and the wealthy at the expense of ordinary people.

Only time will tell whether the Great Reset is a genuine opportunity for change or just another empty promise. What is certain however is that the world will most definitely change as a result of this pandemic and that we will all inevitably need to adapt.

Impact on the Economy

We may see economic systems repaired and rebuilt by world governments hoping this will help tackle climate change and reduce poverty. We may see more investments of billions of dollars in renewable energy and sustainable industries. This could help reduce the impact of climate change.

We may also see a reduction in global trade, which translates to fewer choices for consumers in practical terms. This could increase local employment opportunities for some people, especially if travel is restricted due to COVID-19 measures and border closures.

Changes to the economic sphere could significantly impact people's lives. More people may be working from home if businesses choose to downsize their offices or encourage employees to work from home after the pandemic ends. This could be good news for parents who want to spend more time with their children, but it could also lead to growing isolation and loneliness.

Impact on Our Mental Health

Combined, the stress of the pandemic, the economic downturn, and social distancing have taken an immense toll, even on the most well-adjusted among us. So, it's no surprise that many people are looking to the Great Reset as a way to address and remedy these issues.

The concept of the Great Reset is still in development, but it essentially refers to a fundamental change in the way we live, work, and interact with one another. This could involve everything from rethinking our relationship with technology to changing our priorities as a society.

While it's still too early to tell how the Great Reset will impact our mental health, there's reason to believe it could be a positive one. The Great Reset could help us emerge from this difficult period with a renewed sense of purpose and hope for the future by allowing us to reassess our values and find new ways to connect.

Impact on Our Relationship with Nature

For generations, humanity has been slowly but steadily encroaching on nature. We have decimated forests, dammed rivers, and built cities and highways that fragment ecosystem and displace wildlife. Our relationship with nature has become one of exploitation and ferocious dependency, where we treat the natural world as a resource to be used rather than cherished.

These recent years have been a wake-up call, as we have seen the devastating effects our disregard for nature can have on our health and well-being. The Great Reset provides an opportunity to rebuild our relationship with nature. We can reimagine our cities as green spaces supporting local wildlife, replanting forests, and restoring damaged ecosystems. By working alongside nature rather than against it, we can reverse the damage and start to ensure a more sustainable future.

Impact on Globalization

The Covid-19 pandemic has profoundly impacted the world economy, one of the most noticeable changes being the slowdown of globalization. Multinational companies were forced to re-evaluate their supply chains, and most countries have imposed some form of restrictions on travel and trade.

In light of these developments, it is understandable that many observers have begun to speculate about the possible death of globalization. However, it is worth noting that the current situation is not without precedent. The world economy has undergone similar disruptions in the past, and each time, it emerged stronger than ever before. There is no reason to believe the Great Reset will be any different. The current crisis will likely lead to a more sustainable form of globalization, with a greater focus on local production and a circular economy model.

As we emerge from this period of apparent chaos, remember that globalization is not the end goal but rather a means to an end. The goal should be to create a more prosperous world that is just for all, not to simply facilitate the flow of goods and services imposed by stale and outdated economic dogmas. With this in mind, the Great Reset presents an opportunity to build a smarter and more inclusive future for all.

Impact on Our Priorities

With Covid-19, we've had no other choice but to re-evaluate our priorities as a society. In the span of a few months, we went from competing in the rat race to being forced to slow down and take stock of what truly matters to us.

For many people, this has been a time of introspection and reflection. We had to confront our own mortality, which has led us to reassess our values and life priorities. For some, this meant reconsidering their study or career choices, while for others, it was spending more time with family and friends.

The Great Reset allows us to rethink our priorities and build a better horizon collectively. One key priority is to create jobs that are both meaningful and sustainable. This involves investing in essential sectors like renewable energy, healthcare, and education. It also means supporting young entrepreneurs and small business owners.

Another key priority is to build resilient supply chains that can withstand global shocks. This means diversifying our supplier base and investing in local manufacturing. Finally, a focus on inclusion and social justice is essential. This means ensuring everyone has a fair chance to participate in the economy, regardless of race, gender, orientation, or other discriminating factors. We can build a stronger, more resilient world by building bridges and resetting our priorities.

A Plan to Rebuild the Global Economy

In essence, the goal of the reset is to create a more sustainable and inclusive economy that addresses the world's social and environmental challenges at large. It is not a specific blueprint for action but rather a set of principles that should guide the world's economic, financial, monetary, and institutional policy-makers.

Some key principles of the Great Reset include shifting from carbon-intensive industries to cleaner forms of energy, a move towards digital technologies, and the creation of jobs that help improve people's lives. While the Great Reset is still in its early stages, it has already begun to gain support from many world leaders (including Joe Biden and Justin Trudeau) and worldwide organizations. If successful, it could be a transformative force for good in the world economy.

The Great Reset aims to develop a more sustainable, inclusive, and resilient global economy. It is an ambitious and far-reaching proposal that will require the cooperation of governments, businesses, and civil society. The Great Reset is not a silver bullet, but it is a necessary first step in the right direction. Building a better future for all will be possible with the right policies and long-term investment strategies.

As we've seen, the Great Reset is the name of a global campaign to reset the economy after the COVID-19 pandemic at a time of great societal changes. The campaign is led by the World Economic Forum and billionaire Klaus Schwab, the forum's founder. It is a transnational movement focused on reshaping global economies, changing how people live and work, and ending social inequality. In the upcoming chapter, we'll examine the economic aspect of the Great Reset, namely, how it impacts the mechanisms of the economy and its actors.

Chapter 2

The Economic Aspects
of the Great Reset

The Great Reset Theory suggests that major reforms are needed across society to correct imbalances and achieve lasting prosperity. The theory has gained traction in recent years as income inequality, and other economic issues have become more apparent.

The Great Reset will involve a radically different redistribution of wealth, a fundamental rethinking of our economic model, and massive investments in social programs, education, and infrastructure. While some believe the Great Reset is necessary to save our economy, others believe it is too disruptive to do more harm than good.

Regardless of your stance on the matter, it's clear that the upcoming Big Reset is a complex and controversial issue with far-reaching ramifications. In this chapter, we examine the economics of the Great Reset and how it will affect our savings, investments and pensions. We'll also explore how businesses will be affected, collective priorities, and what opportunities there are for entrepreneurs.

The Impact on Savings and Investments

Global financial markets have undergone major fluctuations since the Coronavirus crisis. The Great Reset is already underway, and the consequences will be far-reaching. While many believe the worst of the pandemic is over, its impact on the economy will likely be felt for years to come.

For starters, let's explore how the Great Reset will impact our savings and investments.

Low-Interest Rates

Interest rates around the world have been in decline for the past decade or so. In the United States, the Federal Reserve has kept rates at near-zero since the 2008 financial crisis. In most of Europe, rates have been negative for some time, meaning states and financial institutions could borrow and get paid for it. The Great Reset is likely to further depress interest rates as central banks seek to stimulate economic growth.

This context of low-interest rates presents challenges for savers. It becomes difficult to earn a decent return on cash deposits. In parallel, for retirees who rely on income from their investments, low rates mean they'll have to take on more risk to maintain their current standard of living.

The good news is there are still opportunities to earn a decent return on your investment, even in a low-rate environment. One option is to invest in dividend-paying stocks. Many companies have a history of paying out a portion of their profits directly to shareholders. Another option is to invest in real estate. While prices have come down in some markets, others continue to experience strong growth.

Market Volatility

The Great Reset is likely to generate more volatility in financial markets. This is because the transition to a new economic system will be fraught with uncertainty. For example, we don't know how countries will react to the new global order. Will they tend to cooperate or compete? How will this affect international trade and investment flows?

The volatility will also be driven by the massive levels of debt around the world. As central banks print money to finance government stimulus packages by the billions, this will lead to inflation, eroding the value of debt and cause investors to demand higher interest rates. All this market uncertainty will make it difficult for savers and investors to achieve their financial goals. However, there are still opportunities for those who are willing to take on extra risk.

Moreover, the Great Reset will have a major impact on businesses. Many will fail and shut down, while others will have to adapt to a new reality. This will create even more uncertainty for investors. In times of market volatility, it's important to maintain a long-term perspective, and attempting to time the market is often a losing prospect. Instead, focus on creating a solid diversified portfolio that can weather the storm.

Inflation

When prices start to rise, inflation erodes your purchasing power and jeopardizes your financial security. The Great Reset is likely to bring higher inflation. This could have a significant impact on your purchasing power, savings, and investments.

The key to weathering inflation is to have a diversified portfolio. This means investing in a mix of assets, including stocks, bonds, and real estate. This will help safeguard your purchasing power and ensure you can maintain your standard of living. You'll also need to make sure your income stream is inflation-adjusted if you're retired. This can be done by investing in inflation-protected securities, such as Treasury inflation-protected securities (TIPS).

To protect yourself from inflation, you'll need to invest in assets that are likely to gain in value over time. One option, as mentioned, is to invest in real estate. While prices have come down in some markets, others continue to experience skyrocketing growth, particularly in large urban centers. Another option is to invest in commodities like gold and silver. These have a history of outperforming other asset classes during periods of high inflation and uncertainty.

Economic Inequality

The Great Reset will likely exacerbate global economic inequality. This is because the transition to a new model for the economy will favor those who are already wealthy and have access to owning capital. The rich will get richer at the expense of the poor, who will see their situation considerably deteriorate.

This inequality will have several negative consequences. For one, it will lead to higher levels of social unrest and political instability. It will also hamper economic growth, as the poor will earn less and therefore have less money to spend. Finally, it will make it harder for people to move up the economic and social ladder.

The best way to combat inequality is through government policies like progressive taxation and social safety nets, which the current order is actively trying to eradicate. But the Great Reset is likely to reduce government spending as countries try to reduce their debt levels. Paradoxically, this will make it harder to combat inequality.

Protectionism

The Great Reset is likely to reintroduce protectionism on a global scale as countries try to safeguard their economies from international competition. This is because countries will be focused on rebuilding their economies and providing jobs for their citizens. So, they'll be less interested in cooperating with other countries, which could lead to a decline in trade and foreign direct investment. It could also lead to a rise in prices, as imported goods become more expensive.

Protectionist measures can hurt the global economy, leading to slower economic growth and higher unemployment. It will also make it harder for businesses to operate in global markets. Consumers may also have a difficult time accessing certain goods and services as a result.

To prevent protectionism from becoming dominant, countries will need to cooperate. This will require an unprecedented level of political and economic coordination. It's also important to keep in mind that protectionism is often driven by short-term considerations, whereas in the long run, it's usually counterproductive.

The Impact on Businesses

The Great Reset is being driven by several factors, including the rise of emerging economies, the expansion of innovation and technology, and the changing demographics of the workforce.

While some businesses have been slow to adapt to these changes, others have embraced them and are thriving as a result.

The businesses that have been most successful in the Great Reset so far are those that were able to identify and leverage new opportunities. For example, many traditional manufacturing companies are now turning to 3D printing to create custom products quickly and efficiently. Other businesses are finding success in marketing their products and services to new customer segments or by providing innovative solutions to address pressing problems.

In many ways, the Great Reset is just beginning, and it remains to be seen how businesses will continue to adapt in order to survive and thrive in this new world paradigm.

Disruptions to Businesses

The Great Reset will inevitably cause disruptions to businesses around the world. Some businesses will be forced to close, whereas others will adapt their products and services to meet the needs of a changing market. The pandemic has already significantly impacted businesses across most economic sectors, and the Great Reset will only intensify these changes.

The most disruptive changes will be felt in the workforce. The pandemic has accelerated the trend of automation, and they will eventually replace many jobs that can now be done by machines. This will seriously affect businesses, especially those that rely on low-wage workers. In addition, the changing demographics of the workforce will require businesses to adapt their products and services to cater to the needs of an aging population.

The Great Reset will also disrupt supply chains. As the global economy is increasingly interdependent, businesses rely on each other for raw materials, components, finished goods, and more. Disruptions at any stage of the supply chain can cause ripple effects that are felt around the world. The pandemic has already highlighted the fragility of global supply chains, and the Great Reset will only exacerbate this problem.

Finally, the Great Reset will have a major impact on businesses' balance sheets. Many businesses have been struggling to survive during the pandemic, and the Great Reset will only make this worse. The upcoming recession will cause a decrease in demand for goods and services, which will lead to a sharp decline in revenue and profit margins. This will put even more pressure on businesses to cut costs and find new sources of revenue.

Invariably, the most successful businesses will be those that can adapt smartly to the new landscape. For example, many companies now focus on providing online services that can be delivered remotely. This has allowed them to continue operating during the pandemic, reach new customers, and stay afloat financially. Other businesses are geared toward developing new products and services that meet the needs of a changing market.

The Great Reset will present both challenges and opportunities for businesses in the global economy, and those that can adapt will thrive in the new landscape.

The New World of Work

The Great Reset will profoundly reshape the world of work. Technology is making it possible for people to work from anywhere, and the global economy is creating new opportunities for businesses to succeed. As a result, the traditional 9-to-5 workday is becoming a thing of the past, giving way to newer and better-adapted arrangements.

It's worth noting that the rise of the "gig economy" is one of the most disruptive changes currently taking place in the world of work. The gig economy is built by independent workers that work on short-term projects or tasks. This arrangement is often made through dedicated freelance online platforms.

This model is growing rapidly, and it is estimated that by 2025, 43% of the workforce will be involved in some form of gig work. This trend is being driven by several factors, including the increasing use of technology, changing demographics, and the rising cost of living.

The gig economy is changing the way businesses work in unprecedented ways. In particular, it makes it easier for them to find workers with the skills they need for specific projects and schedules. As a result, companies can now get work done faster and cheaper than hiring traditional employees.

Ultimately, the Great Reset will usher in a new world of work where employees will become more flexible and businesses more global. This new paradigm will bring many challenges, but it will also provide people with new opportunities to build successful careers. With the right preparation and mindset, the Great Reset is an exciting update time for everyone.

The Impact on Pensions

A recent study by the World Economic Forum found that the world economy will rebalance over the next decade. This new start will have a major impact on pensions, as many will retire earlier than planned. The study suggests the number of people retiring before age 60 will jump from 24% to 30%.

The reset will also lead to changes in how pension funds are managed and administered. For example, more pension funds will go to sustainable and responsible investments. This is because the reset will bring about a fundamental shift in values, with a greater focus on environmental, social, and governance (ESG) factors. As a result, pensions will become more resilient to economic shocks and better equipped to meet the needs of an aging population.

Defined Benefit Plans

The Great Reset will also have an impact on defined benefit pension plans. These are pension plans that provide a guaranteed level of income throughout retirement. The pension's value is determined by several factors, including the employee's salary, years of service, tax bracket, and age of retirement.

Under a defined benefit pension plan, the employer is responsible for funding the pension. This means employers bear the investment risk, which can be quite significant if the market performs poorly.

In recent years, many companies have been moving away from these defined plans due to the fact they are expensive to maintain and that the employer bears the investment risk. The Reset will likely accelerate this trend as businesses abandon defined benefit pension plans in favor of other types of retirement plans.

Defined Contribution Plans

The Great Reset will also impact defined contribution pension plans. These are pension plans that employees contribute to, and the level of income in retirement is determined by the amount of money that has been accumulated in the pension fund.

Under a defined contribution pension plan, the employee bears the investment risk. This means employees could end up with lower retirement incomes if the markets perform poorly. Despite the risks, defined contribution pension plans are becoming more popular as they offer greater flexibility and are less expensive for businesses to maintain.

As such, the reset will likely further increase the popularity of defined contribution pension plans thanks to these aforementioned benefits for both employers and employees. The Reset will also lead to a change in the way that pension funds are invested, where a significant portion will go toward sustainable and responsible investments.

Opportunities for Entrepreneurs

As the world starts to recover from the pandemic, many businesses look for ways to bounce back from the last year's setbacks. The Great Reset provides an opportunity for entrepreneurs to reimagine the way they do business and build a more viable future. By making conscious choices about how they operate and self-manage, entrepreneurs can create positive change in the world.

The Great Reset is a chance to build a fairer, more inclusive economy that benefits everyone. That means that businesses will focus on creating value and not simply turning and accumulating profits. It also means finding new ways to cooperate with other businesses and organizations instead of competing with them.

If you're a self-starting entrepreneur or a small business owner, the Great Reset is an opportunity to turn over the table and make a difference in the world. But it's also a challenge. You'll need to be creative, adaptable, and willing to take risks to succeed. So, are you up for the challenge?

New Business Models

The Great Reset will introduce a fundamental shift in how businesses operate. To succeed in the new economy, they will need to adopt new business models that are more sustainable and inclusive. Many companies are turning to new strategies that are better suited to the current environment. For example, the rising popularity of online shopping has led to a boom in e-commerce, while the proliferation of remote work has created valuable chances for businesses that facilitate virtual collaboration.

Looking ahead, it is clear that the Great Reset will continue to reshape the business landscape in the years to come. As companies adapt to a new reality, we can expect to witness even more innovative business models emerge. The businesses that thrive in the new economy will be those that can innovate, adapt, and set clear priorities.

The Circular Economy

One of the most defining aspects of the Great Reset is the transition to a circular economy. In a traditional linear economy, resources are extracted from the earth and used to manufacture products that are sold to businesses and consumers. Once the product is no longer needed, it is discarded as waste. This linear production model is unsustainable in the long term, as it puts strain on the environment and depletes finite resources.

In a circular economy, resources are reused and recycled as much as possible to avoid wasteful habits. This model is more environmentally sustainable as it reduces the need to extract new resources from the earth. It is also more efficient, as it prevents resources from being wasted, therefore saving tens of billions of dollars on a yearly basis.

The shift to a circular economy will have a profound impact on businesses. Businesses will need to adopt circular business models to succeed in the new economy. Many companies are already starting to explore these alternative models, with practices such as product-as-a-service and waste-to-energy.

The Sharing Economy

The sharing economy is another aspect of the Great Reset that will significantly impact businesses worldwide. In the traditional liberal economy, businesses compete with each other to sell products and services to consumers. Businesses cooperate to share resources, create value, and promote sustainable growth in the sharing economy.

As the name suggests, the sharing economy is based on sharing resources, such as cars, homes, and skills. This model of production is more efficient than the traditional linear economy, as it reduces the need for businesses to own, exploit, and maintain their resources.

As the sharing economy slowly makes its mark, we see a new breed of businesses built on cooperation, not competition. These companies are focused on creating value, not just making money for a privileged few. The most successful companies in the sharing economy are those that can build trust with their customers and create a hope-inspiring community around their business.

As a matter of fact, the transition toward the sharing economy is already in motion. Companies such as Airbnb and Uber have disrupted traditional businesses, such as hotels and taxi companies. In the future, we can expect the sharing economy to keep growing and profoundly reshape how businesses operate.

All in all, the Great Reset will have a great impact on everyone's savings, investments, and pension plans. On a positive note, the shift to a circular economy will create new business opportunities for entrepreneurs. To take advantage of these opportunities, businesses will need to embrace circular business models and adopt a more inclusive mindset. They will need to favor sustainability over short-term gains. With the right approach, the Great Reset can be an opportunity to build a fairer and better-performing economy.

Chapter 3

The Social Aspects
of the Great Reset

The world is on the verge of an unprecedented reset. The old ways are no longer working, and we are being called upon to create a new way forward. This new way will require us to rethink every aspect of our lives, from how we live and work to how we relate to one another.

We must consider how the great reset will impact our social lives and relationships as we enter this new era. In this chapter, we set out to explore the social aspects of the great reset, namely how it will impact our relationships, families, and communities. We will also explore how we can use the Great Reset to create a more sustainable world.

The Impact on Relationships

The Great Reset will have a profound effect on our relationship, to say the least. As our lives are reshaped, we need to rethink what we want from our relationships and how we can best support each other. As the pandemic has forced many of us to change the way we live and work, our relationships have also suffered. With many of us now working from home, we have had to adjust to spend more time with our partners or family. With social distancing measures in place, we have had to find new ways to connect with friends and loved ones. The Big Reset has changed the way we interact, but that's not necessarily a bad thing. Some experts have argued that the pandemic has given us a unique opportunity to reshape our relationships. By focusing on our connections with others, we can be stronger and more connected than ever before.

The Impact on Family Relationships

It goes without saying that the Great Reset significantly impacts family relationships across the world. The current economic and social turmoil has led to increased stress in households and strained interpersonal ties. Many families had to grapple with financial troubles, including unemployment, precariousness, and mortgage foreclosures.

At the same time, many people increasingly rely on technology as they spend much of their time at work or taking care of household responsibilities remotely. As a result, families began to spend less time together in person, communicating mostly over text, e-mail, social media, or Zoom.

However, despite these challenges, the Great Reset also instilled a sense of community among families that had long been fractured by distance and the difference in schedules. In particular, the rise of online social media and messaging apps helped families stay connected even when they couldn't be physically near one another.

Perhaps most importantly, even with mounting pressure in daily life during this period, many families maintained strong bonds and remained close through the hardship. Thanks to their resilience and determination, it is clear that family relationships can flourish even during times of great change rather than crumble under pressure.

The Impact on Work Relationships

The Great Reset has had a tremendous impact on the work sphere and our professional relationships. In a recent survey, over 90% of respondents reported that their work relationships had been affected in some way by the technological boom brought about by the Great Reset.

Many people cited a sense of disconnect from colleagues, both human and robotic, as a result of increased automation and smart algorithms in the workplace. Others pointed to more collaborative teams, enabled by innovative tools such as cloud-based platforms and virtual meeting spaces.

At the end of the day, whether your work relationship style is more individualized or communal, there's no denying that the Great Reset has significantly changed how we view ourselves about those around us. It has enabled us to recalibrate our priorities. So, let's embrace these changes together and make our workplaces thrive in this new era!

The Psychological Aspects of the Great Reset

As the world begins to recover from the pandemic, there's been a lot of talk about the need for the Great Reset. Essentially, this represents an opportunity to re-find our systems and structures to build a more just and sustainable future. It's also a chance to return to "normal" and put the pandemic behind us. Regardless of where you stand, it's clear that the Great Reset is having and will have a major impact on our lives. And one of the most important aspects of this change will be the psychological impact.

As we weigh options and make choices about our future, we will be forced to confront some difficult questions. What do we want our world to look like? What are we willing to sacrifice to make that happen? And most importantly, how will we deal with the inevitable anxiety and uncertainty that accompany change? These are not easy to answer by any means. However, if we want the Great Reset to be successful, they are questions we must grapple with.

Needless to say, that the psychological aspects of the Great Reset will differ from person to person. That said, there are common themes we can all expect to experience. Here are a few of the most important ones:

Anxiety and Uncertainty

The Great Reset will undoubtedly bring about a great deal of change, and with change comes uncertainty. We don't know what the future holds, and that can be a scary prospect. This uncertainty can prompt feelings of anxiety, which can impair our mental and physical health. It's perfectly natural to feel anxious and uncertain when confronted with major life changes; it helps to remember that change can be good. It can bring new opportunities and help us to grow in ways we never thought possible. So, instead of letting pessimism take over, let's focus on the positives of the Great Reset. What new things might we learn? What doors might open for us? How can we use this opportunity to become the best version of ourselves? When we approach the Great Reset with an open mind and a positive attitude, there's no telling what we will be able to achieve.

Loneliness and Isolation

Arguably the most widespread impact of the reset has been the sense of loneliness and isolation felt by millions of people across the globe. For those who have lost loved ones, jobs, or homes, the feeling of being alone with grief can be overwhelming. Many communities that relied on close-knit social connections now find themselves struggling to rebuild these bonds in a significantly altered environment.

While the current state of loneliness may seem bleak, we must remember that it is only temporary. As each crisis passes, we will again find ourselves forging new friendships, opening our homes to loved ones, and rediscovering our sense of belonging in this ever-changing world. So let us not give in to despair but instead focus on every positive aspect we have to gain from this difficult time.

The Fear of Failure

One of the biggest challenges we faced during the Great Reset was the fear of failure. While the precise nature of this change is still unfolding, it is clear it will have a profound impact on how we live and work. For many people, the prospect of such radical change can be daunting, and understandably so. The fear of failure is a natural response to an uncertain future.

With so much doubt clouding our lives, it's natural to feel we're constantly walking on eggshells. We second-guess our decisions, worry we're not doing enough, and wonder if we're up to the task of creating a better future. Failure is a part of life, and it's something all of us must face at one point or another. It's simply a learning opportunity that can help us grow and become better versions of ourselves.

The Great Reset presents both an opportunity and a challenge. Embracing change can be difficult, but it can also lead to new, exciting experiences. The key, again, is to keep an open mind and a positive attitude. With these qualities, you will be well-positioned to take advantage of its opportunities.

The Sociological Aspects of the Great Reset

While the term "Great Reset" has been used in a variety of contexts, it generally refers to a widespread shift in social norms and paradigms. This can be a positive or negative change, but it is typically seen as an overhaul that alters the way society functions. The term is often used to describe moments in the history of significant change in the power structure or social order. For example, the Industrial Revolution was a great reset that dramatically changed the way people lived and worked.

There have been calls for another great reset in response to various societal problems such as climate change, income inequality, and political polarization in recent years. While it is unclear if another great reset will occur, the concept highlights the importance of social change and the potential for society to reimagine itself.

The Impact on Social Structures

Over the past year, the world has undergone profound and redefining changes. The pandemic has upended social norms and disrupted traditional ways of life. In response, many individuals and organizations are now embracing the concept of the Great Reset, a shift towards greater sustainability, inclusivity, and fairness.

While the Great Reset is still unfolding, it is already transforming social structures as we know them today. For example, work-life balance has become a top priority for many people, as remote working arrangements have made it possible to achieve a stable work-life balance. In addition, there has been a renewed focus on concrete environmental issues, as the Great Reset has highlighted the need for greater sustainability.

Finally, diversity and inclusion have become core values for many organizations, as the reset has emphasized the importance of making everyone feel included and valued.

The Impact on Social Interactions

The Great Reset has significantly impacted social interactions, both online and in real life. This new era of instant communication and effortless connectivity has made it easier than ever to stay in touch with friends, family, and acquaintances around the world.

With the click of a button, we can now share moments from our lives almost instantly with people we care about. In parallel, however, this "always-on" mentality can also have negative effects on our relationships. When our time is split between work and online socializing, and we constantly feel pressured to check for new updates and messages, it can, paradoxically, leave us feeling lonely or disconnected from others.

Overall, while the Great Reset has undeniably transformed the way we live and interact with each other, its effects are complex and multifaceted. What is clear is that social connections are vitally important to our individual and collective well-being and will play an essential role in how we navigate this new era moving forward.

Regardless of how great our online connections may be, nothing quite matches the warmth of a face-to-face conversation. After all, being truly present around others will always trump anything technology can offer.

The Impact on Social Norms

As the Great Reset sweeps across our world, it is redefining even the most consensual social norms and behaviors. For example, the growing availability and convenience of online shopping have started to reshape buying habits and preferences. No longer are people limited to purchasing goods from physical stores within their local community. Instead, they can easily browse through countless options and order whatever they need with just a few clicks. This has changed many people's expectations regarding what is possible and convenient and how quickly products should be available after making a purchase.

At the same time, changes in transportation have also had prominent effects on social behavior. Instead of solely relying on cars for commuting, many people are now choosing to walk or ride bikes more often, therefore reducing urban traffic congestion and air pollution around the globe. This shift towards active modes of transportation has encouraged people to engage in more frequent communication and connection with those around them, bringing down barriers between strangers and strengthening local communities.

While these changes may be challenging at first, they ultimately represent positive advances that will help establish a healthier and more sustainable society for generations to come.

Creating a More Sustainable World

The way we live, work, and interact has been drastically affected by the events of the past few years. In the face of global challenges like climate change and wealth inequality, it's become clear that we need to reset our course. The Great Reset is a movement calling for a more sustainable world, one that puts people, the planet, and collective needs first.

Through initiatives like the Green New Deal, the Great Reset is working to build a fairer and more desirable world. From investing in renewable energy to protecting natural resources, the Great Reset aims to create a more sustainable future for us all. So, let's reset our priorities and build a better world together.

Building Resilient Communities

The main reason of the Great Reset is to build more resilient communities that can withstand the challenges of the 21st century. The initiative was launched by the World Economic Forum in response to the global pandemic, aiming to help countries recover from the economic and social damage caused by the pandemic.

As mentioned, one of the goals of the Great Reset is to create more inclusive and sustainable economies. To achieve this, the initiative is promoting private-sector investment in "shovel-ready" projects that will create jobs and spur economic growth. The initiative is also working to increase access to financing for small businesses and self-starting entrepreneurs.

The Great Reset is also supporting the development of new technologies and business models that will reduce carbon emissions and build a more sustainable future. We can create a better world for everyone by working together, and the Great Reset is our chance to make that happen.

Reducing Our Ecological Footprint

Reducing our ecological footprint is more important than ever as we face the Great Reset. This challenge is especially critical for individuals and organizations with a large impact on the environment. Whether it's making small changes to our daily habits or adopting new policies within our workplaces, there are a million things we can do to protect our planet and curtail our impact on the natural world.

For individuals, this might mean turning off lights when not in use and conserving water by fixing leaks or taking shorter showers. For businesses and corporations, this could mean implementing green energy initiatives or shifting to fully paperless communication systems. In either case, by making a conscious effort to reduce our ecological footprint, we can ensure future generations will be able to enjoy all of the beauty and wonder that this planet has to offer. So, let's rise to the occasion during the Great Reset and take action today for a better tomorrow!

Promoting Inclusive Economics

The recent pandemic has forced businesses and economies around the world to hit the reset button. When rebuilding, we must promote an inclusive economy that benefits everyone, not just the wealthy elite. One way to do this is to invest in job creation and training programs that give people the skills they need to thrive in the new economy. Another way to promote an inclusive economy is to support small businesses and entrepreneurs. This can be achieved by providing funding, mentoring and other resources. We must also work to level the playing field by addressing widespread problems such as corruption, tax evasion and money laundering.

We must also ensure that companies are accountable for the rights and safety of their workers and that they pay a decent living wage. Additionally, we must support youth entrepreneurship, especially in traditionally marginalized communities. Promoting an inclusive economy can create a fairer, more equitable world for all.

Advancing Social Equity

As we enter an era of economic and technological change, focusing on social equity is more important than ever. Whether we are talking about better access to education or creating more inclusive workplaces, tackling the issue of social inequality will ensure everyone can thrive in the challenges of tomorrow.

Many have suggested that shaping a new and just social order will be at the very heart of this historic transition. At the root of all great social movements is leadership – leaders who are not afraid to stand up for what they believe, are willing to speak out against injustice, and work tirelessly to produce meaningful change.

With a clear vision for progress and a determination to succeed, we can advance social equity during the Great Reset. So, let's do our part by getting involved, speaking out, and fighting for those who need help because, in this time of transition, every one of us has the power to make a difference. Together, we can build a future where everyone has a fair shot at success.

This chapter has explored the social aspects of the Great Reset. We looked at how it will impact our relationships, families, and communities. We also examined how we can use the Great Reset to create a more sustainable world. The Great Reset is an opportunity to build a better, more sustainable world for everyone. We can make positive changes in our relationships, families, communities, and workplaces by working together. Now, to make it happen, we need to take action. We must come together to promote inclusive economics, reduce our ecological footprint, and advance social equity. We must also be willing to stand up for what we believe in and fight for the change we want to see.

Chapter 4

The Political Aspects
of the Great Reset

The political landscape plays a central role in shaping the Great Reset, the global paradigm shift that began at the turn of the 21st century. Many of the reset's pivotal moments and turning points were driven by politics, from the rise of social media to shifts in domestic and international opinion and policy decisions. From Occupy Wall Street to Black Lives Matter, grassroots activism is also critical to achieving social change.

At its core, the Great Reset is a political movement. It reflects changing attitudes towards social equality and environmental justice, striving to be more inclusive for all, and to create a more sustainable future for our planet.

As we approach this new era of transition and uncertainty, we must continue to engage in politics at every level (local, regional and global) and use our voices to shape this powerful new vision for ourselves and our world. This chapter will explore some of the key political aspects of the Great Reset, including its impact on governments, laws, and politics around the world. We'll also consider the opportunities and challenges that come with this decisive shift. Ultimately, it is up to all of us to decide what kind of future we want to create collectively as citizens of the world.

The Impact on Governments

The Great Reset is recentering the role of governments around the world. In many cases, governments have found themselves deeply entrenched in economic issues, tasked with saving failing businesses and helping struggling workers in the face of changing economic conditions.

However, as economists have noted, the Great Reset has ushered in an era of great disruption, making it necessary for governments to adapt quickly to keep up with shifting demands from their constituents. This has resulted in several new policy initiatives and major reforms to promote economic growth and safeguard public welfare.

Now, while it may take some time for governments to fully adjust to this new reality, there is little doubt that they must be ready to embrace change if they hope to remain relevant and legitimate in modern society.

The Shift in Power Structures

The world has experienced a major shift in power dynamics in recent years, partly brought on by the Great Reset. This is a period of significant socio-economic change where old institutions and traditional hierarchies are eroding and giving way to newer ones. As a result, power structures at every level, from local communities to global organizations, have become more fluid and decentralized. Now, while this may represent a step backward for many, it also opens up new possibilities for progress and development.

Specifically, the reset has rejuvenated grassroots activism and bottom-up organizing on fundamental issues, from climate change awareness to women's rights. With more people connected than ever before, it has become easier for individuals to unite and instigate change on a large scale thanks to technology.

The New World Order

The world is undergoing a major shift as the Great Reset brings sweeping changes across all areas of society. This new paradigm can be thought of as a new world order, in which old collapsing power structures are being replaced by new ones. While this transition may be challenging and at times frightening, it also presents tremendous opportunities for growth and innovation.

In this new world order, the global economy will restructure itself around ideas of sustainability, shared sovereignty, and social justice. Those multinational corporations who brazenly exploit and trash the earth will be held accountable for their actions, and communities of workers will be guaranteed greater protection. Meanwhile, the power of nation-states will be diminished as transnational institutions assume a more prominent and federalist role.

Ultimately, the Great Reset will lead to a more equitable and sustainable world for all. Change is always difficult, but if we embrace the Great Reset and work together to create a better future, we can have confidence that the new world order will be stronger and more resilient than ever before.

Despite the challenges that lie ahead, we should view the Great Reset not as an end to our way of life but rather as a fresh start for a more prosperous and stable world.

The Role of the Elite

Our elites have played a major role in shaping modern society, and their influence can be witnessed in all areas of our lives. For example, they were instrumental in promoting new technologies like the internet and mobile devices, which have transformed the way people work, communicate, and learn.

They have also shaped the economic landscape, pioneering new styles of management and investment strategies that have driven economic growth and increased prosperity for millions around the world. Perhaps their most significant contribution is their role in initiating the Great Reset.

By embracing humanistic values like diversity and sustainability, the elites were able to generate widespread support for these emerging ideas. At first, these ideas were primarily championed by environmental groups and grassroots movements, but political leaders started taking action as they gained more legitimacy in the public eye.

Today, we see progressive policies being enacted across governments at all levels, from living wage laws to renewable energy initiatives, spearheading this new era of progress. So, while it is clear our elites still wield tremendous power today, they should also be commended for helping to set us on the path towards a brighter future.

The Impact on Laws and Regulations

The Great Reset marks a period of massive change in the global economy, bringing with it new challenges and opportunities. One of the areas most impacted by this economic shift is the sphere of laws and regulations. On the one hand, many longstanding laws are rendered obsolete by rapidly-changing technologies, which forces governments to rethink their regulatory frameworks to keep up with these advancements. On the other hand, new sectors are emerging during the Great Reset, requiring policymakers to work in tandem with companies and entrepreneurs to draft new laws to govern them. All in all, the Great Reset has a profound impact on how nations enforce and adapt to laws and regulations, proving itself a pivotal moment in governance across the globe.

The Shift in Economic Power

Since the mid-20th century, the world has witnessed a great shift in economic power. This shift can be attributed to a series of events that began with World War II and led to fundamental global trade and production changes. During this time, traditional economic hubs like Europe were decimated by war and hardship, giving rise to new centers of power in Asia and other emerging regions.

Today, countries like China, India, Brazil, and Indonesia are the ones shaping the global economy. Given their vast natural resources and abundant labor force, this trend does not seem likely to change anytime soon. So, whether you're a business owner looking for new markets, or an investor seeking growth opportunities, it's clear that we live in an increasingly dynamic and interconnected world driven by the forces of change known as the Great Reset.

The Shift in Social Power

Today, one of the most significant changes in the shift in social power that's taking place is due to the Great Reset. For centuries, power has traditionally been held by a small group of people at the top of society. But thanks to the Great Reset, that's starting to change.

In fact, more and more people have access to education, technology, and opportunities that were once out of reach. As a result, they gain influence and become leaders in their communities.

This results in an equal distribution of knowledge and power, which benefits society as a whole. The Great Reset is still unfolding, but it's already impacting the social landscape in major ways.

The Shift in Political Power

We have witnessed a significant shift in political power in recent years due to the Great Reset. This reset caused several changes in how the world operates and the distribution of power. One of the most notable changes is the rise of China as a major economic and political player. This translates into less influence for traditional Western powers and results in a multipolar world.

The Great Reset has also led to an increase in global cooperation, as countries have been forced to work together to address shared challenges. This has prompted several positive developments, such as the 2015 Paris Agreement on climate change. However, it remains to be seen how far this trajectory will last and what other impacts the Great Reset will have on the world's political landscape.

The Impact on Politics

Nowadays, many political systems rely on outdated and ineffective models that are no longer fit for purpose. For example, party politics, the issue of campaign financing, and other opaque practices in reality often lead to corruption and cronyism. The great reset provides an opportunity to rethink the way politics works and to create a system that is apt for the 21st century. This could involve changes to the way elections are conducted, more frequent recourse to local referendums (like in Switzerland and California), and the introduction of new platforms such as participatory budgeting.

It's also worth noting that the Great Reset will likely impact the way we govern ourselves. In an increasingly interconnected and interdependent world, it's becoming more and more difficult for countries to be isolated. The Great Reset provides an opportunity to rethink the way we make decisions and establish priorities at a global level and create a more effective, efficient, and inclusive system of governance.

While it is still unfolding, it's impossible to predict the exact outcomes the Great Reset will have on politics. However, what is certain is that the current and upcoming challenges will profoundly redefine the face of societies across the world.

The Rise of Authoritarianism

One significant and perhaps alarming aspect of the reset is the rise of authoritarianism. These regimes are characterized by strict controls on society, the suppression of dissent, and often aggressive foreign policies. We have seen authoritarianism crop up in countries like China, Russia, Turkey, and Egypt in recent years. Even Europe is witnessing a sharp rise in far-right political ideas and nationalist affinities (Hungary, Poland). This trend is likely to continue as the Great Reset progresses.

The resurgence of authoritarianism is due to several factors, including increasing global economic inequality, the proliferation of new mass surveillance technologies, and the weakening of democratic institutions. For that reason, as the Great Reset unfolds, we are likely to witness the implementation of stricter freedom restrictions in many places across the globe. This could have grave consequences, such as the further erosion of civil liberties, a surge in human rights abuses, and the further widening of economic inequality. It is also likely to cause major conflict and instability, as authoritarian regimes are often aggressive and expansionist. The rise of authoritarianism is one of the most worrying aspects, one we must all be aware of as it progresses inexorably.

The Decline of Democracy

The great reset will also likely have a major impact on democracy. No one could have predicted the modern rise of authoritarianism. While there are many complex factors at play, some analysts point to the increasing globalization of our economy as a key comprehension factor. The global economy has led to the rise of transnational corporations, the weakening of national governments, and flagrant economic inequality. All these factors have contributed to the decline of democracy around the world.

To compete on an international level and keep up, developing nations have had to compromise their democratic principles. The result is more autocratic governments that are less responsive to their citizens' needs and demands. Nevertheless, there is still hope for more inclusive governance as more citizens push back against these undemocratic trends. With new technologies that enable us to share information faster than ever before, we can work together to restore our precious democratic ideals.

The Great Reset provides a rare window of opportunity to reassert the power of democracy, which is the rule of the people, by the people, and for the people. We must collectively work toward a more democratic global economy and strengthen the institutions that safeguard democracy.

The Impact of the Great Reset on Global Governance

The Great Reset is likely to have a profound impact on global governance, the process by which we make decisions at a global level. Effective governance is essential to ensure the world economy runs smoothly and in harmony. The reset will impact global governance in several ways, including the rise of new global institutions, reforms of existing ones, and the emergence of new rules and regulations.

For starters, the most significant impact is likely to be the rise of new global institutions. The great reset will give birth to new institutions to manage the global economy and regulate the activities of transnational corporations. These institutions will be charged with reshaping how the world is governed, and they will be vital for the global economy to run smoothly.

It will also lead to the reform of existing global institutions. It will make them become more responsive to the needs of the global economy and the demands of citizens. As a result, we are likely to witness meaningful reforms in the United Nations, the World Bank, and the International Monetary Fund. Finally, the Great Reset will give birth to new rules and regulations that will have a profound impact on the way the world is governed and will be vital for ensuring global economic and political stability.

Opportunities and Challenges

The Great Reset is one of the defining events of our age. This emerging period of transition marks a turning point in the way we conceptualize politics and society, with major opportunities and challenges arising from new ideas and technologies.

In particular, the widespread adoption of technology has allowed governments to communicate directly with their citizens. Politicians can use social media platforms and online tools to engage with voters, sharing news and information that was previously inaccessible or difficult to find. However, these technologies also make it easier for politicians to spread fake news and track individual citizens online, raising concerns over privacy and personal data security.

On top of this, political campaigns are continually facing new pressures as national borders are becoming less relevant in an era of global connectivity. Whether through migration flows or economic dependencies, countries all around the world are becoming increasingly interconnected. To succeed in this environment, politicians must be prepared to address both local and global concerns that affect us all. In other words, as we stand on the brink of political renewal, there are both huge opportunities and major challenges ahead of us. Whichever path we take will depend on how willing and ready we are to embrace change.

The Need for a New Paradigm

Looking back at the history of human civilization, it is clear we are living through a period of major change and transition. The Great Reset has witnessed many long-held institutions and systems fundamentally disrupted or completely overturned. This shift in the global political paradigm presents both challenges and opportunities for those seeking to make their mark on the world.

While the old centralized power and control model is quickly fading, some are already laying the groundwork for a new era of decentralized politics and governance. These innovators recognize that traditional top-down approaches simply don't work in an age of rapid technological advancement, growing citizen activism, and shifting demographics. Instead, they are looking to build community-led grassroots networks that give a voice to all members of society.

At the same time, newer models will have to account for environmental concerns, rising CO_2 levels, pollution, and declining natural resources. As we move forward into this new world, it is clear we need to start thinking about politics in entirely new ways. Only by embracing change and innovation can we create a truly progressive political paradigm that meets the needs of our rapidly evolving society.

The Possibility of a Positive Outcome

Many are rightfully concerned about what the future may hold after the Great Reset, but there is reason to believe its political outcomes could be positive. Despite the disruption caused by the collapse of key infrastructure and financial systems, this period of chaos could open the gate to a new level of global, more intricate cooperation.

After all, much of what has driven tensions between countries in recent years was financial order. With a common need for resources and support, new collaboration channels will likely emerge. Furthermore, the technological advances achieved during the Great Reset could pave the way for more efficient and equitable systems going forward.

While no one knows what will happen as we venture into this unpredictable era, it seems likely that political outcomes within individual countries and on a global scale could ultimately yield positive change.

This chapter explored the political aspects of the Great Reset. We have examined how it will impact our governments, laws, and politics at large. We have also explored the opportunities and challenges that come with the Great Reset.

As we enter this new era, it is clear that traditional approaches to governance and power are no longer reliable. To meet the challenges of our rapidly changing world, we must be willing to embrace change and innovate in every aspect of our political lives. Only by doing so can we hope to create a more just and equitable society.

Chapter 5

The Spiritual Aspects
of the Great Reset

As we live through these unprecedented times, it's becoming more important than ever to stay centered and grounded. The events of the past years have rattled us to our cores, and it can be easy to succumb to fear and uncertainty. However, if we take a step back and remember our true nature, we can see this time as an opportunity for growth and transformation.

The Great Reset is a chance to realign with our highest selves and create a new world based on love, compassion, and respect. It's an opportunity to let go of the old ways and embrace a new way of being. By approaching the Great Reset from a place of spiritual awareness, we can co-create a more beautiful, harmonious, and sustainable world.

This chapter will explore the spiritual aspects of the Great Reset. We'll look at how it will impact our beliefs, values, and spirituality. We'll also explore how we can leverage the Great Reset to create a more meaningful life.

The Impact on Beliefs

The Great Reset marks a major turning point in the history of human beliefs. Before this momentous event, people naturally assumed the world would continue to develop and evolve along a predictable path. But, as we now know, that is far from the truth. With the Great Reset came sweeping changes across every facet of society, from politics and the economy to science and religion. And perhaps most significantly, it changed our beliefs about what was possible to achieve.

In a way, it ushered in a new era of possibility, showing us that anything can happen if we dare to dream and fight for what we believe in. Moreover, it is truly a blessing that future generations will enjoy the benefits of all these changes, but in other ways, it comes with equally great responsibility, one we must honor by working hard and staying true to our ideals.

If there is one thing the Great Reset is beginning to teach us, it's that no matter how chaotic things may seem, change is always right around the corner. And that's what makes a living through this pivotal moment so invigorating and inspiring. Even in the face of uncertainty and risk, we are building something new and exciting as we forge pathways that will bring about a more just and sustainable future for all.

The Dangers of a Technocratic Worldview

The potential dangers of technocracy (the rule by technology) have become increasingly apparent in recent years. With the advent of the Great Reset, an unprecedented technological shift has upended many aspects of human society, and people are now more reliant on complex algorithms and digital systems than ever before. As a result, we run the risk of losing touch with reality and becoming overly focused on performance and data at the expense of our personal experiences.

This inherent techno-centrism can be disruptive to our communities, as well as to our psychological well-being. We need to remember technology is only one part of what makes us human and that we must strike a careful balance between using it for our benefit and allowing it to overwhelm our lives. In doing so, we can avoid some of the pitfalls associated with a purely technocratic worldview.

Rejecting the Transhumanist Agenda

Transhumanism is a movement that seeks to use technology to enhance human abilities and extend life. Some transhumanists believe that we should eventually merge with technology, becoming cyborgs or even digital beings. However, there are many transhumanist agendas that seek to redefine human existence as we know it. One reason for this is the Great Reset.

The Great Reset is believed to erode personal freedom and privacy. In a world where our every move is tracked and monitored, it's easy to see how transhumanism could be used to control the masses. As a result, many people are rejecting the transhumanist agenda in favor of preserving their humanity.

The Need for a Spiritual Awakening

As the world goes through the Great Reset, it is more important than ever to have a spiritual awakening. Feeling lost and confused is all too easy with so much change happening. However, by reconnecting with our spiritual selves, we can find guidance and understanding. A spiritual awakening can enable us to see the world in a new light and find our place in the midst of chaos.

It can also help us connect with our higher power and tap into a source of wisdom and strength that we may not have realized we had. Ultimately, spiritual awakening will allow us to weather any storm and emerge from the Great Reset as better and more enlightened individuals. The time for a collective spiritual awakening is now.

The Impact on Values

Generally speaking, values are the beliefs about what is desirable, worthwhile, and important in life. Common values include family, friends, health, education, success, wealth, and happiness. During the Great Reset, many people focused their attention on achieving these values to lead a more meaningful life. For example, some have devoted more time to their families, while others have worked harder to achieve success and happiness in their careers. However, it has become apparent that these values do not lead to true fulfillment.

Instead, we must focus on more intangible values like compassion, social justice, and self-growth. The reset will require us to rethink our ways, values, and priorities. For example, we will need to value human life and preserve the environment above economic growth. We will have to prioritize community over individualism and cooperation over competition. Adopting sustainable and equitable practices will also be a challenge we'll need to tackle head-on. The Great Reset is an ambitious plan, but it is essential if we want to create a better world for future generations.

The Balance between Individualism and Community Spirit

There's been much talk about the need for a "Great Reset" in our society in recent years. The basic idea is that our current systems are unsustainable and that we need to apply major changes for the future. One identified area of improvement is our focus on individualism. According to some, our obsession with individuality is one of the main reasons we're facing so many problems today. They advocate for the need to start valuing community and cooperation over competition and self-interest.

There's no doubt our society could benefit from more community spirit and cooperation. However, individualism also has its advantages. It allows people to pursue their dreams and goals, encouraging creativity and innovation in the process. So, while there may be some truth to the critique of individualism, it's also important not to throw the baby out with the bathwater. Ultimately, we need to strike a balance between individualism and collectivism if we want to create a better future.

The Rise of Collectivism

Speaking of which, the Great Reset has begun to redefine the way humans think about collective action. Historically, we have relied on centralized structures and heavily hierarchical systems to perpetuate the society. But in the wake of the recession, we began to witness a renewed focus on community-based resources and grassroots initiatives. This mindset change ushered in an era of what has been called collectivism, where people are more willing than ever before to come together to address pressing issues at the local level.

We can already see how we are improving our ability to effectively respond to economic challenges and environmental pressures. And as long as we remain committed to cultivating communities of support and cooperation, there is no doubt collectivism will continue to be a powerful driving force for good in the world.

The Impact on Human Dignity

Previously, many people were living luxuriously, spending money on things like designer clothes, concert tickets, and fine dining experiences. But as the reset changed our economic landscape and brought about a period of intense consumerism and overvaluation of material goods, it became clear these luxuries ceased to be meaningful markers of humanity. On the contrary, they often encouraged folks to give in to superficial pleasures while neglecting their obligations toward education and self-improvement.

Today, however, we are beginning to rediscover human dignity through more natural pursuits, such as cooking wholesome meals from scratch or cultivating an appreciation for the outdoors. As our culture evolves beyond its fixation with consumerism and status symbols, we can look forward to a new era where people truly value their interconnectedness and their environment. Though it may have cost us some material comforts in the short term, this Great Reset has helped us redefine our priorities and go back to what truly matters.

The Threat to Freedom

While the repercussions of the Great Reset are still unfolding, it has already had a profound impact on freedom around the world. In many countries, restrictions on travel and business have been put in place to combat the spread of Coronavirus. This led to a decrease in global trade and investment and a loss of jobs and jeopardized livelihoods. What's more, many governments have used the pandemic as a pretext to crack down on dissent and erode civil liberties.

The Great Reset has majorly impacted the ideal of freedom, both in terms of the restrictions on individuals and the increased surveillance and control exercised by states. The good news is we have already begun to see a new wave of resistance against unjust restrictions and more transparency from governing bodies. While it is clear the fight for freedom is far from over, the Great Reset has given us a renewed sense of purpose and direction.

The Impact on Spirituality

In this period of significant change, many people are looking for ways to connect with something deeper and more meaningful. For some, this means exploring their spirituality. Whether it's attending online meditation classes, picking up a copy of the Bhagavad Gita, or simply spending time in nature, more and more people are seeking a connection to something greater than themselves.

For many, the Great Reset has been the impulse for this spiritual exploration. With so much uncertainty in the world, many are yearning for a sense of grounding and peace. By connecting with our spiritual selves, we can manage to weather the storm and emerge from this period of a change bigger and more resilient than ever before. If you're looking to explore your spirituality, there are precious resources available online and in bookstores. The key is to find what resonates with you, establish clear goals, and commit to regular practice.

The Dangers of a Digital World

As the world moves increasingly online, there are concerns about how our connection to spirituality will diminish. Despite the many benefits of this reset, there is also a danger we will become too dependent on technology and lose touch with the more metaphysical or intangible aspects of life.

Humans have looked to spirituality for guidance and consolation for thousands of years. In times of turmoil, we have turned to prayer or meditation to find inner peace. Recently, we have become increasingly reliant on technology for information, communication, and entertainment. As a result, we are at risk of losing touch with our spiritual selves.

The Great Reset is an opportunity to reconnect with the things that matter. By reflecting on our values and establishing new priorities, we can ensure our connection to spirituality remains strong in the digital age. The key, again, is to find a just balance between the virtual and the real world.

The Need for Genuine Connection

As the world experiences the Great Reset, it's more important than ever to feel connected to others. Whether it's relatives, friends, or community members, genuine connection is what grounds us and helps us feel supported. Unfortunately, the fast-paced nature of modern life can make it difficult to slow down and connect with others on a deeper level.

With constant distractions and demands on our time, it's all too easy to become disconnected from the people and things that matter most to us. However, by committing to connect with others regularly, we can foster meaningful relationships that enable us to pull through. Whether it's thanks to regular check-ins, sharing our feelings openly, or simply lending a listening ear, genuine connection is the key to lasting happiness and fulfillment.

The Power of Love and Compassion

The Covid-19 pandemic has inflicted tremendous suffering on people all over the world. In the face of this global crisis, it matters more than ever to show love and compassion to those who are most vulnerable, and the Great Reset provides an opportunity to do just that. By coming together to build a fairer, more sustainable future, we can create a more compassionate and just world.

By recognizing and helping those who are most in need, we can help heal the world and make it a better place for everyone. In this time of great challenge, the power of love and compassion can make all the difference.

Creating a More Meaningful Life

As we navigate the challenges of the Great Reset, it's crucial to focus on creating a life that is rich in meaning and purpose. For some of us, that may mean taking a hard look at our career goals and transitioning into something more fulfilling. For others, it could be spending more time with loved ones or pursuing long-neglected hobbies. Regardless of what form it takes, creating a more meaningful life is a worthwhile goal for us all. Fortunately, there are many small steps we can take to get started. So, let's reset our priorities and commit to creating lives that are rich in purpose and intention. It's guaranteed to make the world a better place, and it just might make us happier, too.

Finding Purpose amid Chaos

The recent pandemic has upended our lives in various ways. For many, the past year has been a time of stress and uncertainty. We've had to grapple with big questions about our health, jobs, relationships, and our future. And amid all this chaos, it can be easy to lose sight of what's truly important.

If there's one silver lining to be found in this situation, it's that it can help us to find purpose in our lives. When everything is turned upside down, we have an opportunity to rethink our priorities and make sure we're living by our values. This can be a difficult process, but it's also an incredibly rewarding one. So, if you're feeling lost right now, know that you're not alone, and remember there is always hope for a better future.

Things may never go back to "normal" again, but they can be even better. The purpose is waiting for you on the other side of this Great Reset, and it's time for us all to embrace it. Let's start making the changes we need to create lives that are truly meaningful and fulfilling.

The Importance of Gratitude

There is no doubt gratitude is one of the most precious qualities. When we feel grateful, we tend to be more compassionate, forgiving, and empathetic towards others. This is crucial during times of hardship and transition.

Despite fears and doubts, through a conscious effort to cultivate feelings of gratitude, we can remain focused on our responsibilities, stay hopeful about what lies ahead, and ultimately make a positive difference in our community.

Whether it's taking time to reflect on the small blessings in our lives or assisting those who are struggling, gratitude can help us weather even the most turbulent of times. And as we move forward into an unpredictable future, this simple but powerful practice will serve us all well.

The Transformative Power of Forgiveness

Whether it's the stress of the pandemic, the economic upheaval, or the political divisions, it's easy to feel overwhelmed. But in times of crisis, we also have an opportunity to gather and rebuild. And one of the most important things we can do is learn to forgive.

When we forgive, we let go of anger and resentment, making way for compassion and understanding. We also open ourselves up to new chances and possibilities. Forgiveness can be transformative, helping us move forward in life and create something better. Let's remember the power of forgiveness and use it to build a more compassionate world.

The Journey of Inner Transformation

During the Great Reset, many of us find ourselves facing profound inner transformations. Whether we realize it or not, this inner journey is a reframing process that brings us closer to our true selves. Along the way, we come to gain a deeper understanding of our fears and hopes, as well as the misunderstandings and blind spots that have held us back in the past.

We also begin to cultivate new habits and perspectives that allow us to fully embrace the present moment and live more mindfully. Ultimately, this process grants us the strength and clarity we need to move forward into the unknown with confidence and grace, bringing about lasting change both within ourselves and in our world.

So, if you're on a journey of inner transformation during the Great Reset, remember that every step you take brings you a little closer to who you truly are deep down. And when it's all said and done, you'll emerge stronger than ever before. Remember to be patient and kind to yourself along the way. You deserve it.

During the Great Reset, many of us will embark on a transformative journey of inner growth and personal change. This process can be both challenging and rewarding, but ultimately, it will bring us closer to our true selves. As we move forward, let's remember the power of gratitude, forgiveness, and inner transformation. This will help us weather the storm and reemerge as better people.

It's crucial we stay connected to our values and what truly matters to us. The Great Reset provides a unique opportunity for that as we cultivate gratitude and forgiveness while embracing inner transformation. Let's make the most of this age-defining time to create a better world for all.

Chapter 6

The Practical Aspects
of the Great Reset

With the world in such a state of flux and uncertainty, feeling consumed by fear and panic is a natural response. Now, what if, instead of fearing the future, we embraced it? The Great Reset is not about giving up, it's about rising above our old ways of thinking and being and creating something new together.

It all starts with how we think. After all, we can't change how we act in the world without first changing what's going on in our heads. Through which prism do you choose to interact with your life? What do you believe about yourself, other people, and what's possible for humanity?

The Great Reset is about taking action. It's about creating a world where we all live and work in harmony with nature and each other. This chapter will explore the practical aspects of the Great Reset. It will discuss how to change our thinking, develop our skills, and take concrete action for a better world.

Mental Preparation

We can prepare ourselves mentally for what's to come in various ways. One key strategy is to communicate openly with those around us so that we don't feel isolated or overwhelmed when the reset begins. It's also helpful to spend time in nature, whether by exploring new places or simply spending time around sunshine, trees, and plants.

This helps us remember our roots and connect more deeply with the earth, which in turn will keep us grounded during any period of transition. With preparation and self-care, we can all face the Great Reset with an open mind and a positively conquering attitude.

Finding Your Emotional Equilibrium

If you're like most people, the past year has been a rollercoaster of emotions. From the initial shock of the pandemic to the stress of isolation and uncertainty, it's all been hard to endure. Now, as we enter a new phase of the pandemic with vaccines becoming available, it's more important than ever to find emotional equilibrium. Here are a few tips to help you find your balance during the Great Reset:

1. Make time for self-care. To maintain your emotional health, set aside time for activities that make you feel good. Whether it's going out for a walk, taking a yoga class, or simply enjoying a few moments each day to relax and breathe deeply, making self-care a priority will help you stay grounded during these turbulent times.

2. Stay connected. One of the best ways to manage your emotional health is to stay connected with loved ones, even if it's just through virtual means. Whether you're catching up with friends via FaceTime or spending time with relatives at home, staying connected will help you feel supported and loved.

3. Be mindful of your thoughts. It's easy to get caught up in negative thinking, especially in times of stress. But if you're not careful, negative thoughts can become a self-fulfilling prophecy. So, instead, make a conscious effort to stay optimistic and focus on thoughts that make you happy. This will help you maintain a more positive outlook on life.

4. Seek professional help if needed. If you're struggling to cope with the stress of the Great Reset, don't hesitate to

consult a professional. There's no shame in admitting you need help, and a therapist can provide you with the tools and support you need to get through this ordeal.

5. Remember that this, too, shall pass. The Great Reset may seem overwhelming, but it will eventually become the new norm. By adopting a more mindful approach to the present and focusing on what matters most, you can face the challenges ahead pragmatically and peacefully. The future may look uncertain, but it's important to remind yourself of the bigger picture.

Developing a Positive Outlook

Despite all the challenges of the past few years, remember that we are resilient and adaptable creatures, and we have faced hardships before. The key is to maintain a positive outlook and focus on what we can do to make the best of the situation.

This Great Reset is an opportunity to hit the reset button on our lives and enact the changes we've been looking forward to. It might be a chance to finally start that business you've always dreamed of or to reconnect with nature and your community. Whatever it is, approach this time with a positive outlook, and see it as an opportunity for growth. With effort and a desire for collective betterment, we can all make this a time to remember.

Anticipate Setbacks

The Great Reset is an ambitious effort to re-imagine and rebuild our world after the COVID-19 pandemic. While there is much to be optimistic about, we must also anticipate and plan for potential setbacks. One significant risk is that yet another global health crisis could derail the reset. Likewise, we could see a resurgence of nationalism as people grapple with economic upheaval and insecurity. And, of course, there is always the possibility of natural disasters or other unforeseen events that could disrupt our plans.

The key is to prepare ourselves for these challenges and stay flexible and resilient. By anticipating setbacks and being willing to adapt our plans as needed, we can increase the chances of success for the Great Reset. The future is unclear, but we can face it with hope and determination.

Visualizing Success

As we advance into the Great Reset, it's important to keep our eye on the prize. What do we want to achieve as a society? How do we want to be remembered in history books? It can be easy to get caught up in the day-to-day grind and lose sight of our long-term goals. That said, if we take a step back and visualize what success looks like, we can stay motivated and focused on building a better future for everyone.

Now, what does success look like during the Great Reset? For starters, we want a world that is more just and equitable. We want to see an end to systemic inequality, racism, sexism, and homophobia. We want to see a world where everyone has access to quality education, healthcare, and housing. We want to see a world where we work together to protect our planet and its resources. In short, we want a world that is thriving, happy, and sustainable.

Create a "New Normal"

During the Great Reset, we will be called upon to find new ways of living and thinking. To thrive in this brave new world, we will have to define and develop a "new normal," one that supports growth and resilience despite all the changes taking place all around us. At its core, creating a new normal will require tapping into our creativity and embracing a spirit of openness and collaboration.

To build a happier, more sustainable future, we may need to reimagine our relationships with each other and with the planet. This process may be challenging, but it is possible if we remain open-minded and patient as we navigate this period of change. By working together and keeping the optimism alive, we can create a new way of living that allows us to adapt to the challenges imposed by the Great Reset.

Developing Your Skills

The Great Reset is a unique chance to learn new skills and develop your talents. With so much change in the world, being adaptable and open to learning new things is a phenomenal asset. Whether you're looking to improve your personal or professional life, there are plenty of ways to make the most of this paradigm-changing time. Here are a few ideas:

- Use online resources to learn a new skill.

- Take advantage of job retraining programs offered by your employer or the government.

- Enroll in an online course to gain new knowledge or qualifications.

- Join a virtual book club or discussion group to broaden your perspectives.

- Take part in volunteering or community projects that contribute to the greater good.

No matter what you choose, remember that the Great Reset is an opportunity to become the best version of yourself. Embrace the challenge and seize the day!

Make a Plan

The secret to successfully navigating the Great Reset is to develop a solid plan for your personal, social, and professional development. To that end, start by assessing your current skills and knowledge. What are you good at? What do you need to work on? Is there something you've always wanted to excel at? Once you have a better understanding of your strengths and weaknesses, you can start devising a plan to expand your skillset and thrive in the long run.

- Here are some things to keep in mind as you create your plan:

- Set achievable goals that challenge you.

- Make use of online resources, job training programs, and community projects.

- Take advantage of the learning and growth opportunities around you.

- Keep exploring your options, monitor your progress, and use your new knowledge and skills to your advantage.

With a well-thought-out plan, you can maximize your chances for success during the Great Reset. Embrace the opportunities that come your way and work hard to achieve your goals.

Set Goals

Speaking of which, once you have a plan in place, it's time to set some goals. What do you want to accomplish over the next few months or years? Are you looking to improve your career trajectory, learn a new language or skill, or spend more time on self-care? Whatever your goals may be, be sure to set concrete, measurable targets that you can work toward.

Some good tips for goal-setting during the Great Reset include:

- Focus on learning rather than simply acquiring new skills.

- Prioritize goals that help you maintain a positive mindset and build your resilience and self-confidence.

- Stay motivated by tracking your progress, seeking support from others, and rewarding yourself for your achievements.

- Keep your long-term goals in mind as you work toward your short and medium-term targets.

Get Organized

A crucial aspect of navigating the Great Reset is staying organized. With so much change happening all around, it's easy to become overwhelmed and distracted. By taking a few simple steps to keep yourself on track, you can optimize your chances for success.

Some tips for staying organized during the Great Reset include:

- Create a detailed to-do list and break down large tasks into smaller, more manageable steps.

- Prioritize items so you can focus on the most important tasks first.

- Make use of the technology available to you, including task-management apps, to keep yourself organized and on track.

- Find ways to manage your time more effectively and reduce stress, such as by practicing mindfulness or meditation.

- Make sure to get plenty of rest so that you can stay focused and energized.

With the right method of organization and the right amount self-care, you can make the most of this transition period and achieve your goals with flying colors.

Taking Action in the World

While the Great Reset has brought challenges and uncertainties, it also offers many opportunities to contribute to the greater good. Whether you want to volunteer or pursue a new career path, there are countless ways to make a positive impact. The key is to take action and leverage this opportunity to make a difference in the world around you.

Here are some ideas:

- Pursue a new career in a field that helps build a better future, such as renewable energy or sustainability.

- Volunteer your time and skills to local community projects or non-profit organizations.

- Support businesses and organizations that are working to improve the lives of others.

- Get involved in environmental, social, or political advocacy groups and raise awareness about the issues that matter most to you.

- Share your knowledge and experience with others.

You can make a significant difference in the world during the Great Reset, and the most important thing is to take action. With your efforts, you can help build a brighter future for generations to come.

Speak Your Mind

In times of great transformations, people need a sense of stability and community. By sharing your thoughts and ideas, you can provide that sense of security others are looking for. Besides, by taking a stand against discrimination and prejudice, you can create a more inclusive environment for all those affected by the reset. So, don't be afraid to speak up during the Great Reset. Stand up for what you believe in and make your voice heard!

Your words have the power to change minds and bring people together, so use them wisely. Let your unique perspective guide others towards personal empowerment and hope. After all, we need each other now more than ever. Together, we will come out of this reset stronger and truly celebrate our differences rather than let them divide us. And by lending your voice to the cause, you'll play an essential role in shaping a better, more inclusive future.

Resources and Support

The Great Reset is an exciting time of change and growth. For that reason, it is important to have the resources and support you need to make the most of this opportunity. Many organizations and individuals are committed to helping people during the Great Reset. Here are just a few of them:

- The Global Community Foundation is a non-profit organization dedicated to supporting people during times of transition. They offer a variety of resources and programs, including financial assistance, counseling, and career development services.

- The Reset Network is another great resource that offers precious tools and resources for everyone, including an online community, educational materials, and a directory of service providers.

Finally, consider reaching out to your network for support. Friends and relatives can be great sources of encouragement and practical help. Don't hesitate to ask for what you need, and be ready to give in return. The Great Reset is an opportunity for us to come together and support one another, and by working together, the future looks promising.

Identify Your Resources

One thing you can do during the Great Reset is to identify your resources. Think about what you have to offer and how you can use your skills and talents to help others. There are many ways to make a difference in the world, so find the one that best fits you. To get you started, ask yourself:

- Do you have a specific skill or talent you can share? Perhaps you're a great listener, or you have a way with words. Whatever it is, put your talent to good use and offer it up to others who may need it.

- Do you have knowledge or expertise that could be helpful to others? Share what you know with those trying to find their way during this time.

- Do you have a network of people you can rely on? Don't hesitate to reach out to your relatives, friends, and colleagues for support during the Great Reset.

No matter what resources you possess, you can make a positive impact on the world and contribute to building a better future. With a little creativity and determination, you can help others thrive during the Great Reset!

Seek Community Support

Besides identifying your resources, it is also important to seek community support. This may involve reaching out to individuals or organizations who are committed to helping people during the Great Reset. Here are some ideas to get you started:

- Look for local resources in your area. There may be community centers, religious groups, support networks, or other organizations that can provide guidance and assistance.

- Connect with online communities. You will find many online forums and discussion boards that can provide support and advice.

- Seek professional help. If you're struggling to cope with the changes, don't hesitate to seek counseling or therapy.

Remember, you are not alone during this time of change. Many people and organizations are committed to helping others through the Great Reset. Thanks to community support, you can make the most of this time and create a bright future for yourself and those around you.

Nurture Self-Care

Last but not least, nurturing self-care is another practical aspect of the reset. It essentially involves taking care of yourself physically, mentally, and emotionally. Here are some tips to help you stay healthy and happy during the Great Reset:

- **Make time for rest.** Take a break by spending time doing things you enjoy, whether it's taking a walk in nature, reading a good book, or catching up with friends.

- **Eat a healthy and balanced diet.** Your body needs plenty of nutrients to stay strong and in good shape. Eat lots of fruits and vegetables, whole grains, lean proteins, and healthy fats. Don't hesitate to consult your physician or pharmacist for any supplements to complement your diet.

- **Practice stress reduction techniques.** Find ways to relieve tension and anxiety, whether it's through journaling, deep breathing, or meditation.

- **Exercise regularly.** Physical exercise releases endorphins, which have mood-boosting effects. Plus, it's a great way to keep stress at bay and improve your overall health.

- **Connect or reconnect with loved ones.** Spend time with people who make you feel good. Whether it's your family, friends, or even your pets, connect with those who bring joy into your life.

The pandemic has been a wake-up call for many of us, and things are not likely to go back to the way they were. With this in mind, it's time to embrace the Great Reset. This is an opportunity to rebuild our systems from the ground up and make them more sustainable, equitable, and resilient in the face of future challenges.

Fortunately, there are various practical ways we can make the Great Reset a reality. For example, we can start ensuring everyone has access to basic needs like food, shelter, and healthcare. We can also work to build more sustainable supply chains and reduce our reliance on fossil fuels. We can create new policies and regulations that support these goals. While the Great Reset won't happen overnight, if we all commit to making it happen, we can create a brighter future for generations to come.

Chapter 7

Surviving The Great Reset

It can be difficult to grasp how serious the global economic crises we are facing really is. The problem is so enormous, complex, and inevitable that it's hard to precisely know what to do about it. When the world is turned upside down, you need to take stock of what matters and what doesn't and adjust accordingly. One of the most important things is to ensure that you can use your assets when you need to. This means having them both on hand and out of sight.

If you're not prepared, the global economic crisis will be difficult to weather. In this chapter, we'll explore how to survive the Great Reset. We'll look at the steps you need to take to protect your assets and your livelihood. We'll also explore how to create a new life that is meaningful and fulfilling.

Protecting Your Assets

In recent years, many people have been taking steps to protect their assets and prepare for the Great Reset – a major economic downturn that some experts say is inevitable. Whether it is through investing in hard assets like precious metals, buying land in rural areas, or ensuring you have access to cash reserves, there are several ways to weather the potential financial storm.

Protecting your assets during this time will require careful planning and a good deal of risk assessment. While no strategy comes without risks, you can insulate yourself from the Great Reset with the right mindset and plenty of dedication. So, don't wait, and start planning today so that you can secure your assets against whatever the future may hold.

Gold and Silver

In the coming years of the Great Reset, gold and silver will play a major role. These precious metals are essential for maintaining the stability of our financial systems and providing a hedge against inflation. They are also key commodities in the global marketplace, as investors seek to diversify their portfolios with valuable assets. And perhaps most importantly, gold and silver have always been prized for their symbolic importance.

Whether as jewelry or coins, these metals represent wealth and status like no other. As we enter a transformative period in world history, it is clear that gold and silver will play an integral role in the Great Reset. Whether it be through investment or use as a symbol of value, these precious metals will undoubtedly shine bright during this time of change.

Alternative Currencies

As traditional financial systems crumble, alternative currencies are beginning to emerge. Bitcoin, Ethereum, and other cryptocurrencies are becoming increasingly popular as a means to store value and conduct transactions. These digital assets are not decentralized makes which makes them resistant to government control.

While alternative currencies are still relatively untested, there is no question that they will likely play an important role during the Great Reset. However, several community-based currencies are already being used for trading goods and services. These include time banks (where people trade hours of their time instead of money), and local currencies, which can only be used within a specific geographical area.

As the Great Reset follows its course, we will likely see even more alternative currencies emerge. What matters is to stay open-minded and flexible and be willing to explore these possibilities as they arise. By doing so, you will be better prepared to survive the economic storm ahead.

Storing Your Gold and Silver

If you are concerned about the Great Reset and what it might mean for your gold and silver investments, there are several things you can do. First, it is important to keep them as far away from your home or workplace as possible. This means storing them in a professional facility, preferably in a secure vault.

You may also want to consider splitting up your investments to have different valuable goods stored in different locations. This way, if something were to happen to one of your holdings, you would still be able to access the rest of your wealth. With these tips in mind, you can rest easy knowing that your gold and silver investments are fully protected during the Great Reset.

Protecting Your Retirement

When it comes to planning for retirement, protecting your investments is one of the most crucial things you can do. After all, with economic and market conditions changing so quickly these days, no one can predict what the future has in store. The key, then, is to take steps now to ensure your retirement savings are as safe and secure as possible.

This might mean investing in diverse assets like stocks, bonds, and real estate to spread out the risk. It might also mean keeping a close eye on your portfolio and being prepared to make intelligent decisions at a moment's notice. Whatever strategies you opt for, it's crucial to have your retirement fully protected during this period of rapid change.

Be smart about your retirement investments, and you will be able to navigate whatever the future may bring. In the end, that's what truly matters: securing a prosperous financial future you and your offspring can enjoy for years to come.

Protecting Your Livelihood

We're currently going through unprecedented change and disruption in how our economy and societies are structured. During times of uncertainty, it is more important than ever to protect your livelihood and ensure you can weather the storm. There are a variety of strategies that can help to cushion you against the adverse effects of this major paradigm shift. For example, you can start by seeking out new opportunities in growing fields like high-tech or renewable energy.

You can also work on building your resilience by taking care of your health, cultivating your social connections, and fostering good habits like regular exercise and meditation. Ultimately, the key to surviving and thriving in the Great Reset is staying focused on what's within your control while staying alert and adaptable to changes.

Understand the Impacts

The Great Reset is a period of intense social, economic, political, and environmental change. In the years following World War II, new technologies and shifting global and demographic patterns have reshaped the world in fundamental ways. For many people, this upheaval was positive, as it led to more job opportunities and better access to education and resources. However, for others, the

Great Reset was quite steeped in hardship. In particular, many communities were impacted by the loss of lands or jobs due to changes in industry and climate.

Though we cannot predict exactly what will happen during the Great Reset, we must learn from history and begin preparing for potential negative impacts on our survival. Whether it's saving up money for an unexpected layoff or diversifying your skills through online classes, there are many steps all of us can take today to increase our resilience in times of upheaval.

This will help us get through tough times with greater ease and allow us to better contribute to society as it continues to evolve over time. So, let's embrace the challenges ahead and commit ourselves to find creative solutions to whatever life may bring our way. Remember that knowledge truly is power.

Look for New Opportunities

In times of economic change, it's vital to be on the lookout for new opportunities. This could be pursuing a different career path, investing in new technologies, or taking advantage of changes in the marketplace. For example, the growing field of tech provides a wealth of opportunities for those willing to learn and adapt.

Likewise, if you're concerned about the impact of climate change on your local community, you could look into renewable energy or other forms of green technology. By staying alert to the changes around you and committing to lifelong learning, you will be in a much better position to overcome the challenges of the Great Reset.

Whether it is seeking new job prospects or making connections with like-minded people, there are always new things to explore and discover during this time of change. We can thrive during the Great Reset and carve out a brighter future for ourselves and our communities through open-mindedness and exploration.

Create a Financial Plan

To devise a viable plan, start by examining your current financial situation. List your income and expenses. This will help you identify areas where you can cut back or save more. Next, think about your long-term goals. Do you want to retire early? Buy a new home in a sunny state? Start your own business or franchise? Once you know what you're working towards, you can craft a plan to get there.

Start by setting realistic goals and timeframes. Then, break down your goals into actionable steps that you can take now to start off on the right foot. For example, if your goal is to purchase a house within the next few years, you might start by looking into mortgage options and saving up for a down payment. If you're self-employed, you can set aside money each month into a dedicated retirement account.

There are countless resources available to help you with this process. You can find helpful articles, books, and even online software. The important thing is to get started and make sure you have a solid plan in place. With careful planning, you can weather any storm, even the Great Reset.

Consider Alternative Income Sources

In the event of a Great Reset, it is essential to have alternative sources of income. As most people are aware, economic collapse can have devastating effects on the job market, leaving millions unemployed and unable to provide for themselves and their families. To prepare for this eventuality, it is important to consider alternate forms of income that can sustain you during times of crisis.

One option is to invest your time in a skill or hobby that can provide an additional source of revenue in times of need. For example, many are now turning to online businesses or freelance work to make extra money from home. You could also learn and practice gardening or hunting skills that will help you produce food for yourself and your family. By diversifying your income streams and investing your time wisely, you will be better equipped to weather the devastation of the Great Reset and ensure your survival.

Invest in Skills Training

Investing in skills training is one of the best ways to ensure your success during the Great Reset. In today's fast-paced and technology-driven world, it can be easy to get caught up in the rat race, putting your focus and energy on chasing more money or climbing the corporate ladder. However, this mentality will not serve you well during this time of uncertainty. Instead, focus on developing real-world skills that will help you thrive no matter the situation.

Whether it's learning how to build your shelter, cultivating a garden for sustenance, or mastering new tools like power saws and hammers, taking the time to invest in high-quality training will give you an edge over others who are not as prepared. So, if you want to survive and thrive during the Great Reset, make sure to invest your time and effort in acquiring valuable skills that will last a lifetime. You will then be able to pass on that knowledge to younger generations.

Creating a New Life

The Great Reset is the perfect time to start a new life. Perhaps you've always dreamed of moving to the countryside and starting a farm. Or maybe you've wanted to launch your own business venture. Whatever your dream is, now is the time to make it happen. The world is changing, and it's time for you to change with it.

Creating a new life during the Great Reset can be achieved in many ways. You could find a way to live off a plot of land, becoming self-sufficient and energetically and financially independent. Or, you could start a business that provides goods or services people will need during this period of transition. Ultimately, the possibilities are endless for those who are willing to take advantage of this unique moment in history.

Reduce Your Dependency on Utilities

In these uncertain times, strive to become self-sufficient. One of the best ways to do that is to reduce your dependency on utilities. That means generating your own power, collecting your own water, and growing your own food (or at least knowing how to). Of course, that's not always possible, but even small steps can make a big difference. For example, you can put up solar panels to generate electricity, install a rainwater system to collect water, and plant a garden to grow fruits, vegetables, nuts, and herbs.

By taking control of your own needs, you can increase your chances of survival during the Great Reset and beyond. Begin with small steps and work your way up to larger projects. The important thing is to get started and do what you can to reduce your reliance on the grid. So, take a step today towards greater self-sufficiency — it just might save your life and help you survive.

Maintain a Sense of Community

Whenever uncertainty strikes, it's crucial to maintain a sense of community. Whether you live in a small town or a big city, there's always strength in numbers. When we come together and look out for one another, we can endure any hardship. During the Great Reset, we must band together and support one another. By working as a team, we can get through this difficult period and come out stronger on the other end.

The best way to maintain a sense of community is to get involved. Join a local group or organization, volunteer your time, or simply reach out to your neighbors. By showcasing solidarity, we can make sure everyone has what they need to survive and thrive during the Great Reset. So, let's check in on our neighbors, help out those in need, and come together as a community. A better tomorrow is within our reach.

Prepare for the Worst

While predicting the future is impossible, it's always wise to be prepared for the worst. And with the Great Reset upon us, now is the time to make sure you and your family are as ready as possible for whatever may come. Here are a few key things to ensure your survival during the Great Reset:

1. Stock up on non-perishable food items and water. This will help you weather any potential shortages in distribution.

2. Have a plan for how you'll continue to earn an income. Whether it's setting up a side business or stockpiling

savings, make sure you have a backup plan in case your primary source of income dries up.

3. Be prepared to hunker down at home. Have a plan for how you'll stay entertained and connected to the outside world if you're stuck at home for an extended period.

4. Have an emergency kit ready. It should include things like first-aid supplies, vitamin and mineral supplements, a radio, flashlights, and batteries.

5. Keep your stress levels in check. While this is certainly easier said than done, do your best to focus on the positive and stay calm during challenging times.

By following these tips, you can make sure you're prepared for the worst during the Great Reset. By taking action now, your chances of survival will be much greater. So, stay calm, remain positive, and be ready for anything that comes your way.

Plan for Good Times, Too

While it's important to ready yourself for the worst, it's also wise to plan for the best. The Great Reset presents a unique opportunity to reevaluate your priorities and make positive changes in your life. So, don't just focus on surviving; think about what you'll do once the dust has settled. This can be especially challenging given that so much of daily life is out of our control. However, with some foresightedness and proactive planning, we can all make the most of these tumultuous times.

Some key steps include choosing activities that excite and inspire you, preparing your schedule in advance, and staying organized with to-do lists and calendars. In parallel, it is crucial to remain flexible when facing change so that we can adapt throughout this period of upheaval. With these tips in mind, you'll be able to create a plan for the good times during the Great Reset and truly enjoy these exciting times as they unfold!

Stay Optimistic

No matter what challenges the Great Reset brings, remaining optimistic is of the essence. After all, pessimism will only hold you back and make these times even harder to endure. So, focus on the positive, stay hopeful, and remember that better days are always ahead.

While it may be tempting to get caught up in doom and gloom, one must resist this temptation. We all feel weary from the constant upheaval and uncertainty. That said, it's important to stay optimistic during the Great Reset. Things will eventually improve and be stable again, and we'll all be stronger for having gone through this together.

In the meantime, focus on the things you can control, such as your attitude and outlook on life. Choose to see the best in people and situations, and be a force for good in the world. When you do, you'll help make the Great Reset a time of growth and healing for everyone around you.

Build Your Resilience

The pandemic has been a trying time for everyone. But it's also been an opportunity to hit the reset button and rebuild our lives. Here are some steps you can take to build your resilience during the Great Reset:

First, take stock of your current situation and identify what areas of your life need improvement. Are you as fulfilled as you want to be in your current job situation? Do you need to achieve better financial security? Do you want to strengthen your relationships? Once you know what areas need work, you can start taking steps to make concrete changes.

Next, focus on your mental and physical health. Resilient people are typically well-rounded individuals who take care of their mind and body. So, make sure you're getting enough sleep, eating a balanced diet, and getting regular exercise. Adopting a healthy routine will boost your energy levels, improve your general well-being, and make you apt to overcome future challenges.

Finally, surround yourself with a supportive community. Resilient people have a strong network of family and friends they can rely on. If you don't have that right now, there are plenty of online communities where you can find others who are going through similar experiences. Treat every meaningful relationship you have as something sacred.

All in all, the Great Reset will be a time of major change. Protecting your assets, finding ways to stay positive, and building your resilience are just some of the things you can do to survive and thrive in the new world order. With proper planning and goal-setting, you can make the most of this time and come out stronger. So, don't just focus on surviving; start thinking about how you'll make the most of the times ahead!

Chapter 8

Thriving after the Great Reset

The Great Reset will mark a turning point in the histories of nations, communities, and individuals. Many people will find unexpected opportunities to turn their lives around in its wake. While some will be forced to let go of careers they have been stuck in for years and start fresh, others will take advantage of their forced unemployment to pursue long-suppressed dreams and aspirations. For many, this could be the best thing to ever happen to them.

When COVID-19 hit, businesses and schools shut down, offices empty, and people stayed at home. Everything changed in the blink of an eye. Now that we're emerging from the Great Reset, it's not just a matter of getting back to the way things were before the pandemic, but rather, it's a chance to create something better.

We've already seen how quickly people can adapt to newer ways. The digital revolution was already in full swing when the pandemic hit, but businesses were forced to speed up their adoption of online tools. People also are finding new ways to live. Instead of commuting every day, they might work remotely part-time or buy a house in the suburbs with room for a home office.

When "business as usual" is no longer an option, it's possible to take advantage of opportunities for improvement that may have once been overlooked. In this chapter, we'll explore how to thrive after the Great Reset. We'll look at ways to build a new life after the reset and how to take advantage of the opportunities that will emerge. We'll also explore how to create a more sustainable and equitable world.

Building a New Life

Not so long ago, we all lived in relative peace and prosperity. Then, one day, everything changed. The Great Reset struck with force, questioning our ways of life, and leaving many of us reeling. However, it did not destroy us. With faith, determination, and grit, we picked ourselves up and started building a new future for ourselves. And although the journey was challenging, we emerged stronger than ever before.

Now, as we look toward the future with hope and optimism, we can feel confident that our best days lie ahead of us. There is no limit to what we can achieve, thanks to all the new opportunities for growth. From starting a new business and finding a new job to relocating to a new city, the world is our oyster. We just need the courage to grab onto these opportunities and make the most of them.

New Values

In the aftermath of the Great Reset, a lot has changed. People came together in unprecedented ways to support each other, and the values that guided us shifted dramatically. In place of rampant consumerism and greed, we embraced an ethos of community and shared resources. We realized what we have in common is far more important than what sets us apart, and we developed new ways to value and include all members of society.

With this newly found sense of purpose, it became clear that not only could we recover from the hardships inflicted by the reset, but we could also build a better future for ourselves and future generations. Looking back on those difficult days now seems like a distant memory, as if we were two different people leading two different lives.

At its core, our society remains rooted in those fundamental changes prompted by the Great Reset, and there is no going back to how things were. Instead, we must continue forward together as one unified people, celebrating our shared humanity and working to build a better world for all.

New Habits

The pandemic has forced us to change many of our habits, some of which we may have held onto for years. From the way we work to how we socialize, the past year has seen a dramatic shift in how we lead our lives. As we start to emerge from the pandemic, some of these changes will likely stick with us down the road.

Many have found that they enjoy working from home and are no longer interested in commuting to an office every day. Others have realized they don't need to travel as much as they used to and are happy to vacation closer to home. Whatever changes you've made over the past couple of years, take a moment to reflect on what's working for you and what you want to keep doing as we move into a new era.

New Relationships

Since the Great Reset, many people have found themselves wondering what their lives will look like going forward. After all, the world has been turned upside down in so many ways, from the collapse of familiar institutions to the sudden passing away of friends and loved ones. At first, it can be overwhelming to navigate this new reality. However, those who can connect with others find that they are not alone in their struggles and successes.

By forming relationships with others, whether it's a newfound friendship or reconnecting with old acquaintances, people begin to feel connected and supported as they navigate this brave new world. And as these new connections blossom, a sense of hope grows along with them, giving us all something to look forward to in this defining period. So, if you're feeling overwhelmed by life after the Great Reset, don't give up! There is still so much ahead for you, both now and in the future.

New Career Paths

The Great Reset is an opportunity to rebuild our economy in more sustainable and equitable ways. This notably involves creating new career paths that are based on the principles of the circular economy. Since waste is seen as a resource in a circular economy, products are designed to be reused or recycled back into the system. This approach can help diminish environmental pollution and create new jobs in industries such as green tech, recycling, and engineering.

Another way to create new career paths is by investing in eco-responsible infrastructure. This includes projects such as solar panels or wind turbine installations, constructing green buildings, and developing sustainable transportation systems. These initiatives will create new jobs and help combat climate change effectively.

Finally, we can also create new career paths by supporting social enterprises. These mission-driven businesses focus on providing solutions to social or environmental problems. By investing in social enterprises, we can create new jobs while making a lasting positive impact on the world.

Taking Advantage of Opportunities

With the Great Reset still fresh in our minds, it is easy to get caught up in the chaos and uncertainty that seems to be swirling around us.

However, we must keep taking advantage of the opportunities that come during this transition. The Great Reset is a once-in-a-lifetime opportunity to build a better world for ourselves and future generations.

The first step in leveraging opportunities is to stay informed. By keeping an eye on the news and following social media, we can learn about new initiatives and programs being created in response to the Great Reset. We can also stay informed by reading articles and books about the Great Reset, attending webinars and conferences, and talking to experts in our community.

One key opportunity we should all be taking advantage of is the growth of the green economy. This encompasses everything from renewable energy and sustainable agriculture to green building and pollution reduction. We can tackle climate change by investing in the green economy while creating jobs and revitalizing the general economy. Whether it's learning a new skill or pursuing a valuable interest, seizing these opportunities could be the key to building a brighter future for ourselves and our communities.

Starting Over in a New Environment

After the Great Reset, many people found themselves starting over in a new environment. Although this was undoubtedly a difficult transition, it also presented an opportunity for growth and change. For some, this meant breaking old habits and forming new ones, whereas, for others, it meant reconnecting with loved ones or exploring new interests.

Be that as it may, it was clear people were not content simply staying put in their current circumstances. Rather, they looked for ways to embrace their newfound enthusiasm and carve out happiness for themselves in a new world. Despite the challenges and obstacles, they emerged on the other side stronger and more resilient than ever.

In short, starting over after the Great Reset is proving to be not just an ending but also a beginning. One that truly gave life new meaning and purpose. The future may be uncertain, but it's worth looking forward to. And with the right attitude and mindset, we can thrive in our new environment and make the most of this wonderful opportunity.

Utilizing New Resources

The Great Reset is a chance to break free from outdated models and build a more sustainable future. One way we can do this is by utilizing new resources that can meet our needs without damaging the environment. For example, instead of fossil fuels, we can turn to renewable energy sources like solar, wind, and geothermal power.

We can also explore new technologies that help us use resources more efficiently. For instance, by perfecting recycling methods and developing innovative packaging materials, we can greatly reduce the amount of waste we produce (notably plastic). By embracing the Great Reset, we can create a cleaner, healthier, and safer world for everyone.

Likewise, we can look for ways to reduce waste and pollution in our communities. This would involve things like investing in green infrastructure or switching to greener materials and products. In short, by working together to use our resources more responsibly, we can reduce the long-term impact of the Great Reset on our planet.

Staying Positive and Focused

We've all had to adjust the ways we live and work, and it can be easy to feel overwhelmed about the future. We've been through tough times before, and we've always come out stronger. By staying positive and focused on the bigger picture, we can make it through this transition period more resilient than ever before.

Despite the challenges, there were some silver linings. For example, we've had more time to connect with loved ones, explore new hobbies, and appreciate nature and the world around us. As we continue to persevere and work together, we can create a more just and sustainable future for ourselves, our communities, and the generations to come.

Let's not get distracted by the obstacles in front of us. Instead, we must keep our eye on the goal and do everything in our power to make it happen. We owe it to ourselves and to the world we live in to build a better future. The Great Reset is an opportunity to hit the reset button on our lives and create something entirely better. It won't be easy, but we can make it through anything if we stay positive and focused. So, let's focus on the future and remember that we can make anything happen together.

Creating a More Sustainable and Equitable World

Some major changes are in order to build a more sustainable and equitable world. These changes will involve a process known as the Great Reset, which will rebalance economies, the environment, and political power on a global scale. At its core, the goal of this reset is to hold industries accountable for their impact on the planet while ensuring everyone has equal access to vital resources like food, water, and education.

To achieve these goals, governments and citizens alike will need to take action to promote environmental stewardship, encourage innovation in renewable energy tech and green infrastructure designs, and create new wealth distribution and social support systems. The challenges may seem daunting at first, but with strong advocacy efforts by both grassroots activists and top-level policymakers, we can collectively overcome these obstacles and ensure a more just and durable world for future generations.

Raising Awareness of Environmental Issues

In the aftermath of the Great Reset, it is more important than ever to raise awareness of environmental issues. With so many communities devastated and resources becoming scarce, we need to work together to preserve what we have and protect our planet. Luckily, there are many ways to get involved and make a difference.

One key approach is through education. By sharing knowledge on topics such as sustainable energy sources and organic farming, we can guide people to make more conscious choices that benefit them and the environment. The more aware people are of the impact of their actions, the more likely they are to enact changes in their daily lives to reduce pollution and preserve resources.

Another way to raise awareness is through grassroots advocacy. This would involve organizing community cleanup events or pushing for legislation that supports conservation efforts. In parallel, we can use our influence as consumers to drive demand for environmentally-friendly products and support companies that uphold sustainability ideals. In short, with collaboration and cooperation, we can ensure a brighter future for ourselves and the planet after the Great Reset.

Taking Action to Promote Sustainability

Promoting sustainability in the years ahead requires action on multiple fronts. This includes improving our energy infrastructure and adopting new forms of renewable energy, like solar and wind power. It also means reducing our dependence on non-renewable resources that harm the environment.

There is a vital need to address the causes of environmental problems like climate change, biodiversity loss, and pollution. That means moving away from fossil fuels toward clean energy, protecting wild spaces and promoting sustainable agriculture, and supporting policies that put the planet first. We must also make sure everyone has a fair chance to thrive in the new economy, notably with a commitment to building an inclusive economy that leaves no one behind.

In addition to these changes, we must adjust our mindset when it comes to what is possible. We need to think big, and our solutions must be bold. Since we need to challenge the status quo and build a better future for all, the Great Reset provides us with an opportunity to do just that.

Creating New Systems of Support and Wealth Distribution

As we brace ourselves for the Great Reset, there is no doubt we will have to come up with new systems and approaches for building support networks, distributing wealth, and promoting inclusiveness. After all, our current system simply won't be able to sustain itself in a world driven by economic uncertainty and climate instability.

One possible solution is to create more localized economies focused on local production and resource management rather than relying on distant suppliers or factories. By supporting farms, artisanal businesses, and other small-scale ventures that produce goods locally, we can build resilient communities that are less dependent on centralized support systems. We might also explore models of basic income or universal services that provide all citizens with the means to live dignified lives without having to depend on unemployment benefits.

Ultimately, it will take plenty of creativity and out-of-the-box thinking to build truly sustainable systems in the future. But as we face these challenges together, remember there is hope for a new vision of a society where wealth is fairly distributed so everyone can thrive and live in peace.

Supporting Inclusive and Equitable Systems

The Great Reset offers us an opportunity to build a more inclusive and equitable society. We should use this moment to part ways with systems that have enriched a handful at the expense of many. And we can work together to build new systems and structures that support all members of society, regardless of race, gender, class, background, or any other factor.

This will require collaborating on a grassroots level to support diversity and inclusion in aspects of society such as education, business, politics, and the arts. By coming together to stand up for equality, we can ensure no one is left behind as we rebuild our world after this cataclysm. At the same time, we must also challenge outdated beliefs or governance models that reinforce harmful stereotypes and contribute to global inequality.

One way to do this is by supporting local communities and strengthening the sense of connection within our society. When we know our neighbors and have a vested interest in their well-being, we are more likely to treat them with respect and compassion. This, in turn, can contribute to a more equitable society where everyone has the opportunity to thrive.

Taking a Long-Term View

At the heart of these major changes lies a shift in mindset. Instead of focusing on short-term gains and immediate gratification, we must start thinking about the long-term health state of both our planet and our societies and how sustainable they are. This means making decisions that may not be popular at the moment but that will benefit us in the future. It means valuing people and the environment over profits and working together to build a better world.

A crucial part of this process will be embracing uncertainty and change, as well as looking at the big picture rather than getting caught up in day-to-day concerns. With this long-term perspective, we can begin to tackle the challenges facing us today. The Great Reset poses a major challenge to humanity. However, with open hearts and minds, we can rise to the occasion, take on this historic moment, and build a brighter future.

As we approach the Great Reset, it is clear that we are facing unprecedented challenges. Building sustainable and equitable systems will require creativity, compassion, and cooperation. Opportunities to thrive will be available to those who are willing to adopt a long-term view and put the needs of people and the planet first.

As we look toward the future in the aftermath of the Great Reset, creating new systems and structures that support a more inclusive and sustainable society will be the number one priority. This will require profound changes in the way we do things and a shift in our collective mindset. Ultimately though, by working together and looking ahead, we can create a better world for everyone.

Chapter 9

FAQs about the Great Reset

There are many questions about the Great Reset. What exactly is it, and how will it impact our lives? How do we prepare for this monumental event? This chapter will address some of the most frequently asked questions about the Great Reset and provide information and insight that will help you navigate this transition period with confidence. We'll explore the impact of the reset on various aspects of our lives and dispel some of the myths surrounding it.

FAQs about the Great Reset

Whether you're a lifelong learner looking to stay ahead of the curve or simply curious about what's on the horizon, this chapter has something useful for everyone. So, join us as we explore some of the Great Reset's key issues and find out how we can all prepare for what's to come.

How Will the Reset Affect My Job or Career?

Many people are concerned about how the Great Reset will impact their profession or livelihood. The answer depends on several factors, including your industry, your location, and your skillset. For example, if you work in the tourism sector, you may find that there are fewer jobs available now because people travel way less than before. However, if you work in healthcare, you may find more job opportunities as the demand for health services increases.

The best way to prepare for the Great Reset is to ensure you have skills that are in demand. For example, jobs in healthcare and sustainable tech are likely to see increased demand as these sectors grow rapidly in the coming years. You should also consider taking courses or training programs to get a leg up.

Ultimately, the effect of the Great Reset on your job or career will depend on your circumstances and those of your industry. However, by being proactive and staying up-to-date with the latest trends in your sector, you can position yourself to thrive in the changing landscape.

What Does the Reset Mean for My Finances?

The Great Reset is upon us, and it will profoundly impact our finances, one way or another. This shift will not only affect the way we think about money and how we go about earning it but also dictate what we choose to spend our hard-earned cash on. Some of the major changes we can expect to see include more emphasis on financial security over material wealth, increased use of alternative currencies like cryptos, and a greater reliance on cybersecurity.

The Great Reset will be an opportunity to reevaluate our relationship with money and rethink how we manage our personal finances. If you want to be prepared for this new reality, start by taking stock of your current financial situation. This means looking at your debt and assets, as well as your income and expenditures. Once you have a clear idea where you stand, you can begin to make changes that will help you weather the financial challenges of the Great Reset.

Whether we realize it or not, this massive shift has already begun and is sure to have far-reaching and long-lasting consequences. Are you ready for the Great Reset? Only time will tell, but one thing is clear: it's never too early to start preparing.

How Will the Great Reset Change My Lifestyle or Quality of Life?

The Great Reset is a time of great uncertainty and change, but it will also bring exciting opportunities for those that are best prepared. From new technologies that will revolutionize how we live and work to shifts in our social and economic structures, the Great Reset will have a profound impact on our lifestyle and quality of life.

One of the most significant changes we can expect to witness is an increase in the use of digital technologies. This means more individuals will be working remotely, and there will be greater demand for new products and services that enable us to stay connected and productive.

Another key component of the Great Reset will be a renewed focus on sustainability and environmentalism as we work to find solutions to our most pressing challenges, such as climate change and resource scarcity. The Great Reset may usher in an era of uncertainty, but it will also open new windows of opportunity and pave the way for a more sustainable, equitable, and connected future.

What Is the Purpose of the Great Reset?

The Great Reset is a term used to describe a range of social, economic, and technological shifts that are fundamentally reshaping the way we live, work, and interact. The main drivers behind this reset include rapid advances in automation and artificial intelligence, changing consumer preferences, rapidly shifting demographics, and widening wealth gaps and social inequality around the world.

At its core, the challenge of the Great Reset is to adapt to these profound changes to create greater resilience and sustainability for individuals, communities, and societies. Whether it's by developing new technologies or building more sustainable communities, we must embrace this period of change to thrive in an increasingly uncertain future.

Only with a clear understanding of the purpose of the Great Reset can we begin to prepare our societies for a better tomorrow. The challenges we face are daunting, but they are not insurmountable. With the right mindset and a willingness to embrace change, the future will be promising and definitely worth living.

What Challenges Does the Great Reset Present?

The Great Reset will present many great challenges for individuals, businesses, and governments around the world. Challenges like rapid technological changes and growing inequality between rich and poor nations. In addition, we are already seeing shrinking traditional industries and rising concerns about resource scarcity and climate change.

One of the biggest challenges of the Great Reset will be to manage these changes in a way that guarantees greater resilience and sustainability for our societies. This will require a concerted effort from individuals, businesses, and governments to find new, innovative solutions to our most pressing issues.

Another key challenge will be to help individuals and communities adapt to these changes in a way that is consistent with their values and priorities. This means providing support for those struggling while also encouraging innovation and creativity across all of society.

Despite these challenges, many believe that the Great Reset presents a unique opportunity to build a more desirable future for humanity as a whole. By learning to adapt to our current situation and taking the necessary steps towards smarter and more conscious consumption patterns, we can work together to ensure a better tomorrow for ourselves and for generations to come.

What Are Some of the Potential Benefits of the Great Reset?

The advantages of the Great Reset are many and varied. As we adapt to our changing world, we have the opportunity to create a more sustainable future and build more equitable and inclusive societies.

While the concept of the Great Reset is still evolving, several potential benefits have been proposed. These include a sharp reduction in greenhouse gas emissions, increased social cohesion, and more equitable wealth distribution. Additionally, the Great Reset could lead to better collective mental health and well-being, as well as opportunities for lifelong learning.

Of course, only time will tell if the Great Reset succeeds in achieving these goals. However, it is clear there is a growing need for transformative change, and the Great Reset provides an important framework for moving forward. With the support of individuals, communities, and governments around the world, we can advance toward more inclusive and rewarding horizons.

Is the Great Reset a Good or Bad Thing?

There's no doubt the Great Reset is a major undertaking. It's an effort to re-imagine and rebuild our world in the wake of the COVID-19 pandemic. However, one might ask, is it a good or a bad thing? Some argue the Great Reset is an opportunity to build a fairer, more sustainable world. They point to the fact that our current system has left billions of people behind, and that the pandemic has laid bare its many shortcomings. They also argue that the Great Reset is our chance to build a better future for all.

Others, however, are skeptical of the motives behind the Great Reset. They worry it will lead to more centralization of power and further erosion of our civil liberties. Only time will tell whether the Great Reset is a force for good or not. That said, one thing is certain: it's a historic moment, and we will all be shaping its course. The choices we make today will have repercussions for years and decades to come.

What Are the Implications of the Great Reset for the Future?

As we look to the future, the implications of the Great Reset are becoming increasingly clear. By changing our patterns of consumption and production, we have begun to disrupt many aspects of the global economy. This led to shifts in how we work and interact with one another. For one, it has become easier for businesses and individuals to collaborate on projects via digital platforms and social media. At the same time, however, these changes have contributed to the rising income inequality and environmental degradation.

As we navigate this new reality, a number of important questions must be addressed. How can we find stable employment in an ultra-dynamic job market? How do we reconcile technological advances with privacy and data security concerns? And perhaps most importantly, how do we ensure all people enjoy the benefits of economic growth without being left behind? While there is no definite answer to these big questions, it is clear they will shape the course of our future down the road.

How Can I Prepare for the Great Reset?

The Great Reset is a historic opportunity to open a new chapter and rebuild our world for the better. Now, what does that mean for you and me? How can we make sure we're prepared for it? Here are a few things to keep in mind as we head into this new era:

1. Be open to change. The world is evolving rapidly, and we need to be able to adapt to those changes. Whether it's a new job, a new system of governance, or moving to a new country, embrace the change and make the most of it.

2. Be flexible. We don't know what the future holds for sure, so it's important to be adaptable. Things may not go according to plan, but if we're open to change, we'll be able to roll with the punches and still come out ahead.

3. Be positive. This is a time of great opportunity, so focusing on the positive and what we can achieve will only drive us forward. There's no room for negativity or pessimism. We must dedicate our energy to making the world a better place for everyone.

4. Be prepared. There's a lot of work to be done, so it's important to be mentally and physically prepared. Keep learning, keep growing, and stay motivated in order to contribute to building a better future.

There's no doubt the Great Reset is a major turning point in the history of humankind. It presents us with significant challenges but also many exciting opportunities. By being open to change, remaining flexible, positive, and prepared, we can make the most of this moment and start looking forward to a brighter future.

Myths about the Great Reset

Although many people have heard of The Great Reset, there are still plenty of misconceptions about what it is. The Great Reset is a term first coined by the World Economic Forum to describe the need for an overhaul of global systems in the wake of the Coronavirus pandemic. The idea is that we need to build back better by making our economies more resilient, inclusive, and sustainable.

However, some people have taken this to mean that the world is coming to an end or that we will all be forced to live in communes. This couldn't be further from the truth. The Great Reset is an opportunity to collectively re-imagine the future and build a fairer, more sustainable world for everyone. So, let's debunk some of these myths and set the record straight.

Myth #1: The Great Reset Is a Globalist Plot

There is a common misconception that the so-called "Great Reset" is nothing but a plot devised by global elites to spearhead their nefarious one-world agenda. While it is true many of these elites do have a vested interest in seeing countries unite on some level, the Great Reset itself is nothing more than a naturally occurring phenomenon driven by complex economic and technological forces.

Proponents of this theory point to economic trends such as stagnant wage growth and an ever-widening wealth gap between rich and poor as clear indicators that businesses and governments must work together to tackle future challenges. What's more, tech disruptors like the rise of automation and global internet connectivity are radically altering our way of life, leading many to conclude there will soon be no going back from this new reality.

How we respond to these changes will ultimately determine if the Great Reset can be embraced as an opportunity or viewed as a threat to our survival. Regardless of what we choose, what matters is we keep an open mind and continue to reflect as we navigate this rapidly changing world. Above all else, let's not let controversy and conspiracy theories cloud our judgment or obscure reality. At the end of the day, one thing is certain: change is inevitable, it is right around the corner, and we will need to adapt to it.

Myth #2: The Great Reset Is a Communist Conspiracy

Contrary to popular belief, the Great Reset is not a global communist conspiracy. Many people seem to think the Great Reset is a sinister plot by some shadowy organization to impose communism worldwide. However, this assumption is based on a fundamental misunderstanding of what it actually entails.

In reality, the Great Reset encompasses our collective efforts to transition away from fossil fuels and other unsustainable energy sources, preserve the health of our environment, and safeguard our future. This process involves various stakeholders at all levels of society: governments, businesses, institutions, and individuals alike all work together towards this shared goal.

It is clear that the Great Reset is not a communist conspiracy. It is a crucial step towards building a sustainable future for all.

Myth #3: The Great Reset Is a Plot by Big Business to Exploit Workers

Many people believe the so-called "Great Reset" is simply a plot by big businesses to exploit workers. This notion is misguided for several reasons. To begin with, it fails to account for how complex and multifaceted the overall economy is. A small change in one area can have ripple effects, which is why we can't accurately predict how the Great Reset will unfold.

Moreover, it ignores the fact that many companies are already investing in new technologies and transitioning to new business models to remain competitive. Finally, it overlooks the wide range of categories who stand to benefit from changes in our economy, including those previously marginalized or underrepresented, such as women, people of color, and members of the LGBTQ+ community.

We should embrace it as it is an opportunity to create a better future for everyone.

Myth #4: The Great Reset Is a New World Order Scheme

Many are tempted to believe that the Great Reset is part of some larger scheme by powerful elites to create a New World Order. While it is true, the reset has significantly reshaped politics, economics, and societies around the world, this idea seems far-fetched and overly conspiratorial. After all, what possible motivation could these elites have in instigating a global crisis? Certainly, they stand to lose as much as anyone else in the event of widespread collapse and chaos.

At best, it seems likely they are simply responding to a situation over which they have limited control. Throughout history, several major powers have always been vying for dominance at any given time. And in an unstable world where conditions are constantly evolving and shifting, one of these powers may simply be taking advantage of an opportunity to advance its interests.

Whatever their motives may be, the idea of a secretly orchestrated plot behind the Great Reset is nothing short of a myth. Ultimately, we must rely on ourselves and our communities to navigate this difficult period. Though we will face challenges along the way, it is through our actions that we can reshape our ways of life and build a better tomorrow.

Myth #5: The Great Reset Is a Hoax

Lastly, some people believe the Great Reset is a hoax, whereas others see it as a real and imminent danger. While some see this as a necessary response to the many challenges we face, others view it as a plot from above to seize more power and control. No matter where you stand on the issue, it's important to be informed about what's being proposed. Only then can you make up your mind about whether you should support or oppose it.

The term "Great Reset" broadly describes several important economic, social, and political initiatives. Some of these initiatives are real and have already been implemented, while others are merely proposals. The most notable examples include the World Economic Forum's "Great Reset" initiative, whose aim is to promote the development of new technologies that can help address social and environmental problems on a global scale.

Nevertheless, many skeptics have pointed out that the Great Reset is simply a rebranding of existing agendas, such as sustainable development and the green economy. Likewise, others have accused the World Economic Forum of using the reset as a pretext to push for more global governance. While there is certainly some truth to these criticisms, the Great Reset is still a very real and significant phenomenon.

Ultimately, it is a complex and wide-ranging initiative that will significantly impact our society and economy, for better or worse. Despite widespread misconceptions, it is vital to understand its fundamental drivers, challenges, and potential impacts on everyone.

Only then can we make informed decisions about how to implement it and the changes that come with it.

As we move forward into the uncertain future that lies ahead, we must remain informed, engaged, and resilient. Whether we choose to reject or embrace it will have major implications for our world. So, we need to make sure that we choose wisely!

Bonus Chapter

The Great Reset in Action

There has been a growing awareness of the need for a global Great Reset in recent years. We need a fundamental shift in the way we live and work in order to build a more sustainable and equitable future. The good news is that this reset is already underway. In fact, around the world, people are starting to reimagine what is possible and are taking action to make their vision a reality.

The Great Reset is already in full swing, from cities experimenting with new ways of organizing public space and businesses reimagining their supply chains to individuals choosing to live more simple lives. The question now is how we can accelerate this process so we can create the future we want to see.

This bonus chapter will explore how the Great Reset is already underway. We'll look at some of the initiatives and projects taking place around the world to help make the reset a reality.

1. Organization of Public Space

The way we use public space is changing. COVID-19 has forced us to rethink how we interact with each other in shared spaces. In response, many cities are changing how their public spaces are organized. For example, Los Angeles has closed off some streets to car traffic so that people can socialize while maintaining a safe distance from each other. New York City is also experimenting with pedestrian-only zones in busy areas.

These changes are part of a larger trend toward the Great Reset, a term that describes how the pandemic is making us re-evaluate our priorities and changing the way we live. It remains to be seen what other changes will come as a result of the reset, but the organization of public spaces will certainly be one of them. With more people working from home and spending less time commuting, the demand for safe, comfortable, and inviting public spaces will considerably increase.

2. Rethinking Business Supply Chains

Over the past few decades, we have seen an incredible transformation in producing, transporting, and selling goods. Old business models and supply chain strategies are becoming obsolete as companies strive for greater efficiency and more sustainable practices. Specifically, the rise of e-commerce has pressured businesses to rethink their supply chains from the ground up.

Now, the Great Reset is not just about reimagining logistics or streamlining distribution. It's about strategically changing our mindset when it comes to how and where resources are used. At its heart, this Great Reset involves a shift away from narrow efficiency goals towards broader sustainability goals.

As such, businesses must learn to look beyond short-term profitability and focus on building long-term value through collaboration. This means prioritizing sustainability at every stage of the supply chain instead of viewing it as an added cost or obstacle. To do so effectively, companies must embrace new technologies, adapt to change, and open up new avenues of collaboration with their partners, suppliers, customers, and communities.

In other words, for businesses to succeed in this rapidly changing landscape, they must be willing to truly reinvent themselves. Whether by leveraging smart automation solutions or innovative technologies or by simply adopting a more holistic and collaborative approach to business, the companies that thrive in the years ahead will be those that can adapt and evolve.

3. Reskilling the Workforce

As the pace of technological and industrial transformation accelerates, we are witnessing an unprecedented shift in the skills workers need to succeed in the modern economy. For example, with rising automation and artificial intelligence, a growing number of jobs are becoming obsolete. At the same time, new jobs are being created that demand expertise in areas such as data analysis, software engineering, and digital marketing.

This transition requires a major reskilling effort on the part of both employees and employers. Fortunately, many initiatives have been launched to enable workers to transition into these new roles, from retraining programs at local colleges to personal online coaching services. Reskilling the workforce may be one of our best chances of thriving in the coming years. After all, those individuals who have access to relevant training will be well-positioned to succeed in our ever-changing economy. The sooner we tackle this challenge, the sooner we can build the collective future we want.

4. Supporting a Green Recovery

As the world begins to recover from the pandemic, there is an opportunity to rebuild in a more sustainable and equitable way. The Great Reset is a call to action for businesses, governments, and society at large to work towards a better future. One key part of this reset is supporting green recovery, which entails investing in clean energy, green infrastructure, and nature-based solutions. It also means creating new jobs in sectors like renewable energy and sustainable agriculture. A green recovery will help us build a more resilient world that can withstand future shocks and ensure a more just and prosperous future for all.

5. Harnessing Technology for Good

The key to changing the world for the better often lies in leveraging the latest technological advancements. Thanks to major strides in artificial intelligence and machine learning, we are now able to solve problems and address challenges that were previously inaccessible or even inconceivable. One clear example of this is found in green technology: by using high-tech materials and energy storage solutions, we can reduce our environmental impact and create a cleaner and more sustainable future.

In parallel, innovations in communication technologies have made it easier than ever for people all over the world to collaborate and pool their resources towards a common goal. Whether it's developing new sustainable energy sources, combating climate change, or advancing medical research, technology has the power to be a game-changer when it comes to creating a better future. So, let's harness its power wisely and keep working towards making our planet a brighter place for everyone.

6. Strengthening Global Institutions

One of the key goals of the Great Reset is to strengthen global institutions, so they are better equipped to deal with and resolve major global challenges. To this end, the World Economic Forum has proposed several measures, including:

- Reforming the UN Security Council to make it more representative and effective;

- Setting up a new global body to tackle climate change

- Establishing a World Health Organization task force on pandemics

- Creating a global financial safety net to protect against economic shocks

- Reforming the World Trade Organization to make it more effective

These are examples of how the Great Reset could help strengthen global institutions. These measures would go a long way in making the world a more stable and prosperous place if implemented.

7. Redesigning the Economy for Purpose

The pandemic has been a wake-up call for many. It highlighted the fragility of our systems and the importance of working together for a better future. The Great Reset is an opportunity to redesign the economy so that it works for everyone, not just a privileged few. By re-founding the economy, we can create more secure jobs, reduce inequality, and make sure our planet can continue to support life.

Essentially, we need to move away from an economy based on endless growth and consumption towards sustainable and equitable one. A sustainable economy meets the needs of present generations without compromising the ability of future generations to meet their own needs. It is an economy that values people and the planet, not one that glorifies personal enrichment and wealth concentration.

To achieve this goal, it is vital to put people's well-being at the heart of our economic system. We need to value care work and environmental protection as much as we value financial gain. We must create an economy that works for everyone and give all of us a chance to succeed.

8. Advancing Sustainable Development

The Great Reset is a chance to accelerate the implementation of Sustainable Development Goals (SDGs). The SDGs are a blueprint for a better world, and they provide a framework for addressing many current and future challenges. The pandemic has shown us the importance of health, education, and gender equality, and the Great Reset is an opportunity to give these objectives the attention they rightfully deserve.

The Great Reset is also an opportunity to address the causes of the SDGs, such as rampant poverty and global inequality. By tackling these issues head-on, we can make progress on all 17 of the SDGs. The Great Reset enables us to build a better world for everyone, and advancing sustainable development is a crucial part of that goal.

9. Tackling Inequality

A key goal of the Great Reset is to reduce inequality, both within and between countries. To achieve this, the reset focuses on three areas: education, employment, and entrepreneurship. In terms of education, the Great Reset is working to ensure that all young people have access to quality education and skills training.

It also focuses on promoting employment and entrepreneurship. By creating more jobs, reducing unemployment, and supporting entrepreneurs, we can significantly mitigate the devastating effects of inequality, both within countries and between them.

Finally, the Great Reset is working to combat gender inequality, which remains a major driver of inequality in many parts of the world. To achieve this goal, we must first address the root causes of gender inequality, such as discrimination and violence. We also need to make sure women have equal access to education, employment, and entrepreneurship opportunities.

In terms of employment, the Great Reset aims to create more decent and dignified jobs. For entrepreneurship, it supports the creation of more inclusive and sustainable businesses. By tackling inequality in these three key areas, the Great Reset aims to create a more prosperous and equitable world for everyone.

10. Building Resilient Societies

Our society at large is approaching a critical pivot point, in which we must make significant changes to avert disaster. While there is debate about exactly how this reset will play out, it is clear we must adapt quickly and efficiently if we are to survive and thrive in the future.

One way we can build resilient societies for the Great Reset is by investing in renewable energy sources and green infrastructure. Not only does this help us lessen our dependence on fossil fuels, which largely contribute to global climate change, but it also fosters greater environmental stewardship and community resilience.

In a similar vein, by promoting public transportation, walkability, carpooling programs, smart growth practices, and other ideas that reduce our reliance on automobiles, we can build more sustainable societies with fewer negative side effects.

11. Creating a More Inclusive World

One of the Great Reset's most important goals is to create a more inclusive world where everyone has an equal opportunity to thrive. To that end, the initiative is promoting gender equality, enclosing the digital divide, and empowering young people worldwide. The Great Reset is also working to build a more sustainable future by fighting climate change and protecting the environment. These are all vital steps towards creating a fairer, more just world.

12. Protecting Our Planet for Future Generations

There is no "planet B," which is why we must do everything we can to protect it. To that end, the Great Reset is committed to resetting our relationship with the planet. We want to make sure we live sustainably and that we're leaving the world in a better state for future generations. There are three key areas to consider if we want to achieve those goals: climate change, biodiversity, and resource efficiency.

Climate change is one of the biggest challenges facing our planet, and we must take urgent action to reduce emissions and stop the damage. Biodiversity is essential for all life on Earth, which is why it must be safeguarded. We're also focused on resource efficiency because we must start using resources sustainably. The Great Reset is all about taking action now to protect our planet for future generations. Together, we can make a significant difference.

The Great Reset is a once-in-a-generation opportunity to shape a better world for everyone. Today, as we witness these changes taking place all around us today, it is clear we have entered a new era of opportunity for building resilient societies. By working as a community and adapting our lifestyles to protect our planet and ourselves from the many challenges ahead, we can ensure a brighter and more promising future for generations to come.

Conclusion

The Great Reset will be over, but the hard work is just beginning. While we'll all be glad to get back to our lives, there are things we can do now to make sure the days ahead are as good as they can be. You might not think it now, but there are valuable opportunities a disaster like this can bring. We can view this as a chance to start anew and create the world we want to see and live in. After all, there's no reason things should go back to the way they were before.

The Great Reset can bring us together. It won't happen overnight, and it will take a lot of effort, but we can build a better future if that is truly our collective aspiration. Hopefully, this book will have given you the tools, knowledge, and information you will need to survive and thrive in these times of profound change.

The first chapter examined what the Great Reset is and how it will affect different aspects of our lives. The second chapter delved into the economic aspects of the reset, including how to protect your finances and how to find opportunities in the new economy. The third chapter looked at the social aspects, including how to stay connected and how to find support.

The fourth chapter considered the political aspects, including how to stay informed and get involved. The fifth chapter explored the spiritual aspects, how to stay grounded, and finding meaning in the new world. In the sixth chapter, we looked at the practical aspects of the Great Reset, including how to prepare yourself and your family for the transition.

The seventh chapter was all about how to survive the Great Reset, with effective steps to protect your assets and livelihood. We also learned how to create a new, meaningful, and fulfilling life. The eighth chapter looked at how to thrive after the Great Reset, with ways to find opportunities and build a better future.

In the ninth chapter, we answered frequently asked questions and dispelled some common myths about the Great Reset, including its impact and how we can prepare for it. And finally, in the bonus chapter, we looked at how the Great Reset is already playing out in different parts of the world. From the Global South to North America, people are making decisions that will shape the world to come.

The Great Reset will inevitably be an enormous challenge, but it's one that we can overcome if we work together. We have the power to build the future we want to see. It's up to us to make this a reality. Now, let's get to work!

Thank you for buying and reading/listening to our book. If you found this book useful/helpful please take a few minutes and leave a review on Amazon.com or Audible.com (if you bought the audio version).

References

Conspiracy theories aside, there is something fishy about the Great Reset. (n.d.). OpenDemocracy. https://www.opendemocracy.net/en/oureconomy/conspiracy-theories-aside-there-something-fishy-about-great-reset/

Corporativa, I. (n.d.). Great Reset: for a healthier, more equitable, and prosperous post-COVID-19 world. Iberdrola. https://www.iberdrola.com/innovation/great-reset

Explained Desk. (2021, January 30). Explained Ideas: What is The Great Reset, and why is it controversial? The Indian Express. https://indianexpress.com/article/explained/what-is-the-great-reset-and-why-is-it-controversial-world-economic-forum-7160434/

Hodgins, M. (2009). The Great Reset. Authorhouse. https://www.weforum.org/great-reset/

Monitoring, B. B. C., & Check, B. R. (2021, June 23). What is the Great Reset - and how did it get hijacked by conspiracy theories? BBC News. https://www.bbc.com/news/blogs-trending-57532368

Now is the time for a "great reset." (n.d.). World Economic Forum https://www.weforum.org/agenda/2020/06/now-is-the-time-for-a-great-reset/

The Great Reset Conspiracy: How it Spread in the Netherlands.
(2021, March 29). Vision of Humanity.
https://www.visionofhumanity.org/the-spread-of-the-great-reset-conspiracy-in-the-netherlands/

the great reset: Latest News & Videos, Photos about the great reset.
(n.d.). The Economic Times.
https://economictimes.indiatimes.com/topic/the-great-reset